The FAMOUS FACES of *INDY'S WTTV-4*

SAMMY TERRY, COWBOY BOB, JANIE & MORE

JULIE YOUNG

THE
History
PRESS

Published by The History Press
Charleston, SC 29403
www.historypress.net

Copyright © 2013 by Julie Young
All rights reserved

First published 2013

ISBN 9781540221698

Library of Congress CIP data applied for.

To all of my television heroes—thanks for everything!

Contents

Acknowledgements

First and foremost, I must acknowledge Peggy Nicholson Powis, who whether she knew it or not inspired this entire project with her cheerful e-mails and a care package that caused the wheels in my head to spin. "Aunt Peg," I could not have done this without you. I am grateful for your friendship and your support, and I am honored to be a part of your extended "family."

To Bob Glaze, Janie Hodge, Matt Hodge, Brian Reynolds, Mark Carter, Bob Carter, Staci Meo, Mindy Winkler, Kathleen Angelone and everyone who had a hand in making this book possible—thank you for seeing the value in this project and being willing to help push it forward.

Thank you to Ray Boomhower at the Indiana Historical Society and Joe Gartrell at The History Press for recognizing the importance of these personalities in the local television market and entrusting me to tell their tales.

Thank you to all of my readers who expressed excitement at this title and told me to "go for it" or contacted me with stories that are included in these pages, including Colleen Foy, Rebekah Whirledge, Alan Hunter, Matt Hodge and Rusty Ammerman. You are the best, and your support means everything to me!

And last but not least, thank you to Chris and Vincent, who show up at every signing, listen politely when I wax poetically about the "good old days" and begrudgingly nod when someone says, "You must be so proud of your mom." You are the two I can lean on through good times, bad times and all the times in between.

INTRODUCTION

Starstruck

My first brush with a celebrity came in 1975, when I was three years old. It was Labor Day weekend, and my parents had read that Peggy Nicholson (host of the *Peggy & Popeye Show* on WTTV-4) and Don Barnes (aka Ronald McDonald) were making a personal appearance outside of the Indianapolis Hyatt Regency Hotel in connection with the annual Jerry Lewis Telethon benefitting the Muscular Dystrophy Association (MDA).

For a young child incapable of making the distinction between a local television host such as Nicholson, a fast-food mascot and a national celebrity like Lewis, this was a major event. In my mind, stars did not come any bigger than Nicholson, who had a daily television show, as opposed to Lewis, who I only saw once a year. As for Ronald McDonald…well, that clown and I went way back, and I spent a good number of Friday nights in one of his fine eating establishments, where his smiling face beamed down at me making sure every meal was a happy one.

There was a block party–like atmosphere near the entrance of the Hyatt, where Ronald and Peggy were holding court and cheerfully greeting everyone in attendance and encouraging folks to make a donation to the MDA "fishbowl." I vaguely remember pointing to the Eagle's Nest Restaurant atop the hotel and asking if the telethon was in there. "Yes," my mother said. It wasn't a lie. The local affiliates and phone banks were inside, but of course I took that to mean that Jerry Lewis and Ed McMahon were inside calling for drum rolls and accepting $1 million checks from the firefighters' union. While I was distracted, Peggy looked over my head to my mother and mouthed, "What's her name?" "Julie," my mother mouthed in reply.

A minute or so later, it was my turn, and I was taken aback when Peggy recognized me, calling me by name and asking me where I had been. "We've been waiting so long to see you!" she declared. Dumbfounded, I watched as she turned her attention to Ronald and announced my belated arrival. Without missing a beat, he too acted as though I was a long-lost friend, relieved that I had graced them with my presence at last. The two fawned over me like I was visiting royalty, and I fell for their act—hook, line and sinker. What little kid wouldn't?

My mother recounted that story several times over the years, but it wasn't until I was older that she came clean about what really transpired that day. Rather than feeling angry at having been made the butt of the joke, I was touched that two people who were complete strangers to me would go the extra mile to make me feel important and act as though they knew me personally. As a regular WTTV-4 viewer, I'm sure I felt like I knew them personally. I watched Peggy's show each and every afternoon as she led her peanut gallery–style audience into the studio, allowing each child to say their name before "grabbing a button" (code for "take your seat") and settling in to watch the day's cartoon offerings. I loved everything about Peggy, from her youth to her enthusiasm, and I knew her wide-eyed "Smo-oo-th Sailing" signoff by heart.

Interestingly, my connection with Peggy did not end on that September day outside of the Hyatt. When I was nine, I wrote my first "fan letter" to Peggy in care of her WTHR-13 show *Peggy and the Vantastics*. She displayed her address at the end of each episode and encouraged her fans to write in. It took me three weeks to write the complete address as it flashed on the screen, and after writing, I was shocked to receive a personal handwritten reply that not only thanked me for my letter but also referenced enough of the content to let me know that the correspondence was read and appreciated. I proudly displayed that letter on my bulletin board for months and remained a loyal viewer of her work across several stations.

A few years ago, I wrote a blog post about that first meeting with Peggy, never dreaming that Peggy herself would actually read it. A friend of a friend had spotted the post and sent it to her. When Peggy reached out to thank me for sharing the memory, it was as if I was three years old all over again. I was so excited to hear from Peggy again after so many years! Very quickly, the two of us became pen pals, and though our correspondence, Peggy shared with me many of her memories of her "magical time" at WTTV when the station was full of engaging television hosts and low-budget, locally produced programming featuring memorable characters. It was those e-mails that became the catalyst for this volume.

Although there were a number of well-known kiddie-show hosts that found their way into the national spotlight—Bozo the Clown, Captain Kangaroo, Mister Rogers, etc.—there were countless names in smaller markets throughout the country that had a big impact on the children of the area. Ask any child who grew up in Indianapolis or Central Indiana in the '60s, '70s or '80s who they watched with any amount of regularity. One station and four names tend to stand out from the rest: WTTV-4's Sammy Terry, Janie, Cowboy Bob and, of course, Peggy. These local personalities played a significant role in the lives of millions, acting as surrogate parents, cool older siblings and understanding friends. Unlike today's generation, which learns its life lessons at the hands of a yellow sponge residing in an oceanic suburb known as Bikini Bottom, our hosts were real; they were local, and we connected.

Day after day, week after week, the hosts of WTTV-4's most popular offerings came into the living room and acted as disc jockeys for favorite Hanna Barbara cartoon shorts or vintage creature features while touting their sponsor's product and making a number of personal appearances around the state. One could run into a favorite host anywhere, including the Indiana State Fairgrounds, Paramount Pizza Palace on the city's eastside, a supermarket grand opening or even a local Burger Chef Restaurant. Each meet-and-greet was a delight for fans who wanted to meet a member of the WTTV-4 gang, and lines often stretched down the block. "My boss and mentor [Channel 4 station manager] Don Tillman once told me that my audience was not only the thirty or forty-five kids sitting in the studio but also the thousands of kids on the other side of the camera lens that I couldn't see," Peggy (now Peggy Powis) said. She said it was important to make every appearance something personal and special for the kids who came out to say hello and to treat every fan letter with the respect it deserved. "Every note and every piece of art I received was logged. I reveled in the repeat writers because I could pull their index card and respond not only to their most recent letter but also to anything they had written in the past."

Parents also appreciated the subtle educational messages promoted in the programs along with the cartoons and silliness even if their children were content to watch their favorite animated characters, hear the submitted jokes, look for their original artwork to be shown and listen for their name. "I remember Janie announcing my birthday on the air," said Christy (Beasley) Herris. "That was such a thrill."

A button with the words "I am a Channel 4 TV Star" was handed out to numerous young television viewers to help them feel that they were part of the show. *Courtesy of Peggy Powis.*

As for the hosts, they were in the right place at the right time, as they struck gold with their programs during an era (and at a station) that was full of creative possibilities. "Those were the salad days," said Bob Glaze. "We had the world by the tail then, but I always knew it wouldn't last forever."

But while it lasted, a good time was had by all—from the starstruck viewers to the hosts, who still marvel at the influence they had over the lives of many and are still willing to share the stories and memories of the legendary characters they created.

CHAPTER 1

The Little Station that Could

The New York World's Fair promised visitors the "Dawn of a New Day" when it opened in Flushing Meadows-Corona Park on April 30, 1939. For 44 million guests who flocked to the gates, many of whom had been affected in recent years by the Great Depression, the wonders and innovations of tomorrow were a dazzling sight. Highlights of the fair included a streamlined pencil sharpener, a keyboard-oriented speech synthesizer, a futuristic car presented by General Motors and some of the earliest television sets. Little did anyone know that the latest and greatest in New Age novelties would be shelved, as factories converted to wartime production only a few months later, but fairgoers were able to get a taste of what was on the horizon.

A NEW MEDIUM

By the time fairgoers saw the television for the first time, it was already a ten-year-old concept. John Logie Baird of Hastings, England, is credited for assembling the first set in 1926, but it wasn't until the World's Fair that the public was able to experience the new medium that allowed folks to "be there when they aren't." In addition to showcasing the box itself, the event offered several transmissions by the National Broadcasting Company (NBC) that featured children's entertainer Burr Tillstrom.

For most, television was a novel concept, but few honestly believed that it could give radio a run for its money. Who would want to watch a ball game at home when buying a ticket and sitting in the grandstand was so much more enjoyable? Sure, the magic box had the "gee whiz" factor, but most felt that it was a passing fad or a luxury that could be enjoyed only by the very rich.

Initially, those naysayers were right. Later that year, when NBC began its regular television broadcasts, the network barely had enough material to provide two hours of programming each week for adults, let alone try to dedicate a significant time to the kiddie viewer. In fact, in the early days of television, network executives didn't see children as their target audience at all. After all, it was parents who had the money, not the kids. Adults were the ones who made the financial decisions in the household and the ones who had shelled out the money on a television unit. Shouldn't networks and independent stations concentrate on family-based programming and focus advertising efforts toward the parents? It sounded like a good idea but by the late 1940s and early 1950s, network advertising executives realized that children were an untapped market, exerting a great deal of influence over what their parents bought. Just as radio shows realized there was potential in a younger audience, networks began to look for opportunities to reach this demographic.

Reaching a Younger Audience

According to Tim Hollis, author of *Hi There, Boys and Girls! America's Local Children's TV Programs*, at a time when networks were limited to primetime programming and a few scattered soap operas during the day, they learned to rely on film packages to fill up time, "especially during the time of day when they were hoping to attract younger viewers." Vintage Western flicks were brought to the small screen and broken up with a live host (usually a station employee or radio announcer) who could read the sponsor's commercials. If he was willing, the individual might don cowboy-inspired clothing and appear before a rustic background (provided the station's budget allowed for it.) "The Western accent was optional," according to Hollis.

It wasn't long before the cartoon and kiddie-show format followed. One of the first was NBC's *Howdy Doody* (1947), which aired on Tuesdays, Thursdays and Saturdays from 5:00 to 6:00 p.m. before its popularity changed its schedule in September 1948 to a daily half-hour show airing from 5:30 to 6:00 p.m.

Howdy Doody featured a marionette puppet in the title role; a cast of human characters, including "Buffalo Bob" Smith, the silent Clarabell the Clown (originally played by Bob Keeshan, who would go on to great fame in his own long-running show Captain Kangaroo); and a studio audience of forty children known as the Peanut Gallery. Not only did the children gamely shout, "It's Hoody Doody Time!" in response to Buffalo Bob's question, "What time is it?" but they also chimed in to sing some of the sponsors' jingles during commercial breaks. Those early advertisers included Colgate, Halo Shampoo, Three Musketeers candy and Poll Parrot Shoes.

The American Broadcasting Company (ABC) was not far behind its competitor when it began the first Saturday morning children's lineup in 1950 with *Animal Clinic*, featuring live animals, followed by a circus-themed show called *Acrobat Ranch*. According to writer Mary Bellis, *Acrobat Ranch* was set against a Western backdrop and featured acrobats such as Tumbling Tim and Flying Flo. During one of the segments, "Uncle" Jim presided over an in-studio competition in which boys and girls from the audience were selected to play for merchandise prizes sent in by network sponsors. Other shows began to dot the small screen landscape as well, including Burr Tillstrom's *Kukla, Fran and Ollie* and *The Small Fry Club*.

Hollis notes that early cartoon packages offered silent and early sound production shorts that were obscure and far from entertaining to most viewers. It wasn't until Disney opened its vault in 1954 to ABC that other studios looked to see what was collecting dust on their own shelves. A year later, the Columbia Broadcasting System (CBS) purchased the Terrytoon library and packaged the animated shorts into *The Mighty Mouse Playhouse*, which ran for twelve years on the network. Warner Brothers would join the fray by year's end, offering Porky Pig and the wisecracking, carrot-chomping Bugs Bunny, with Paramount jumping on the bandwagon in 1956 with Baby Huey, Little Lulu, Herman and Katnip, as well as Popeye the Sailor.

EXPERIENCE WITH CHILDREN OPTIONAL

The cartoon show was easy and inexpensive to produce. Like the Western film fests before, stations relied heavily on an engaging host who was willing to develop a colorful persona and emcee the show. Experience with children or a background in theater rarely mattered, according to Bob Keeshan:

> *Get Charlie, who's the staff announcer. He may not know anything about children, but so what? Let's not spend any money on writers. That's ridiculous. We'll put him in a clown suit or a fireman's outfit, make him a police officer…whatever, and he'll basically wend his way through cartoons. Don't worry about what's in the cartoons. We really shouldn't be too much concerned about that sort of thing. They worked in theaters all through the '30s and '40s, and I'm sure they showed all kinds of what we would now think of as anti-social messages. But they sold, and that's what was important in those days.*

Kiddie shows provided a unique opportunity for former vaudeville and burlesque comics to recycle and revamp old material for a whole new audience. Today, the Internet is ablaze with former kiddie hosts who had nefarious pasts or created controversy on the air. One of the most famous examples concerned Soupy Sales, star of ABC's *Lunch with Soupy* show.

Lunch with Soupy began in 1953 on WXYZ-TV in Detroit, Michigan. It featured slapstick humor, which often resulted in Soupy getting hit in the face with a pie, and the show became so popular that ABC picked it up and gave the Sales show national exposure. However, controversy followed. Live shows, the lack of a seven-second delay and un-vetted scripts resulted in gaffs and gags that outraged parents. Sales made news on January 1, 1965, when he instructed his young viewers to send in those "green pieces of paper with pictures of the presidents on them" found in Mom and Dad's pocket book, and in return, he would send them a postcard from Puerto Rico.

Though it is unknown how much cash was received and later donated to charity by the comic, complaints rolled in, and the host was suspended—only to make a triumphant and unapologetic return to the airwaves a few weeks later. Sales was also accused of telling a "blue" joke on the air, and while the infamous obscenity was never proven, there were times when kiddie hosts offered innuendo-laden punch lines in their material that went over the heads of young audience members—but not their parents.

Raising the Bar

At least one mogul of the time would not allow his material to be showcased on low-budget kiddie shows. Walt Disney realized that television would not only offer him the opportunity to re-run vintage material but that it would also give him the chance to cross promote all of his upcoming film projects, dabble in new technologies and create high-quality, family-based programming. He was a natural at combining cartoons, live action, behind-the-scenes footage and the latest innovations to create long-running shows such as *Disneyland*, *The Wonderful World of Disney*, *The Wonderful World of Color* and *The Mickey Mouse Club*.

The Mickey Mouse Club is a classic example of how Disney used television and a backlog of cartoons to expand his empire. Using local children discovered on playgrounds and in school recitals (no professionals), Disney's crew polished the youngsters into the Mouseketeers who sang and danced, interviewed special guests (which might be a member of the Disney art department or famous actor), showed newsreels, starred in their own serials and introduced a cartoon from the Disney vault. While the kids were the stars of the show, Disney picked staff songwriter Jimmie Dodd and writer/animator Roy Williams to serve as hosts. Former Mouseketeer Annette Funicello said that Disney wanted the show to appear as though it was produced for kids by kids and include content that was both appropriate and informative. "Mr. Disney was adamant that the show not talk down to kids. He felt that if it were aimed at the twelve-year-olds, their younger siblings would naturally start watching anyway," she said.

Syndicated nationally and shown after *American Bandstand* in the afternoons, *The Mickey Mouse Club* was a breakout hit with kids and proved that children's shows could be educational and entertaining at the same time. This led to more academic-based kids' programming in the form of *Ding Dong School* and the syndicated *Romper Room*. However, the prevailing belief at the networks was that sillier was better. Kids preferred Bozo the Clown and Soupy Sales to shows that were blatantly educational. Besides, developing quality programming without the vast resources of Disney took time, and few stations were willing to stick with shows that were slow to build momentum.

When Keeshan pitched the concept of *Captain Kangaroo* to CBS as a morning children's show, network executives were convinced it would never work. However, Keeshan pointed to popular Cincinnati host "Uncle Al"

Jimmie Dodd and Annette Funicello during their days on the original *Mickey Mouse Club*. *Photo © Walt Disney Company.*

as an example of what he hoped to do on his own show. "Uncle Al" was a wildly successful and fast-paced local morning show that boasted a five-year wait list for children hoping to be guests on the program. "It was enormously successful and one of the reasons that CBS took a chance on putting the Captain in that time slot," Keeshan said.

Popular Host, Controversial Content

But a popular host did not always mean a successful show. The content had to hold the viewers' interest, and throughout the 1950s, Popeye was the hottest property in children's television. Parents were less than enthusiastic about the violent images outlined in the shorts, as well as the notion that by eating spinach, one could amass enough muscle to stop an oncoming train. The "Our Gang" shorts, which were a staple on many programs, were often racially insensitive, employed crude humor and ultimately had little relevance to the postwar generations.

Billy Ingram and Kevin Butler penned an article that suggested that the disappearance of the original "Our Gang" shorts had a lot to do with the fact that the children were portrayed as orphans and street urchins of absentee parents, allowed to roam the neighborhood with an unleashed pit bull and interact with any number of vagrants, tramps and other people of ill-repute. "The early shots weren't pretty, but the world was a harsh place during the Depression," the authors note, commenting that Roach's later "Little Rascal" shorts offered slicker production and featured a core cast including Alfalfa, Spanky, Darla, Butch, and Froggy. "The shorts began reflecting a more modern family ideal. As a result, parents were less likely to be depicted as lousy role models."

According to Hollis, in 1954, Columbia Pictures released the first package of shorts containing the antics of The Three Stooges, which took television by storm. While the trio knocked Popeye out of the top spot in terms of popularity and horrified parents everywhere, "as the 1950s melted into the '60s, a new concept in syndicated cartoons began to emerge from the drawing boards," offering a whole new variety of beloved and relatively safe animated friends for young viewers.

But who would bring this material to the masses? It would have to be a station owner or manager savvy enough to comb the building for undiscovered

A vintage postcard for an early WTTV-4 Little Rascals cartoon show sponsored by Chesty Potato Chips. *Courtesy of Peggy Powis.*

Peggy Rhoads
59 S. 24th
Terre Haute, Ind.

talent, harness that energy and allow these protégées to cultivate shows that spawned long-running careers and garnered generations of fans.

Sarkes Tarzian

As the expanded technology for radio continued to improve and the new innovation of television began in earnest, there were a number of people excited for the opportunity to be part of its development. One such man was Sarkes Tarzian, a Bloomington resident, inventor, engineer, entrepreneur and founder of one of the nation's first small-town television stations that became a model for others throughout the United States.

Born in 1900, Tarzian and his family immigrated to America from a small village in Turkish Armenia, settling in Philadelphia, Pennsylvania. As a young, curious and energetic young boy, Tarzian often collected bits of wire and tubes in order to fashion his "finds" into crude radio receivers. His passion for electronic technology stayed with him throughout his childhood, and he ultimately worked his way through the University of Pennsylvania as an ice cream cone salesman before earning his degree in engineering in 1924 (a graduate degree followed in 1927). Once his education was complete, Tarzian accepted a position at the Atwater Kent Company, where he was employed as a radio designer.

Tarzian focused much of his work in those days creating components that could be mass produced instead of individually crafted, ultimately keeping costs low for the end user. His developments led him to the Radio Corporation of America (RCA), where he traveled throughout South America and Europe as a troubleshooter for the company. In 1940, RCA assigned Tarzian to Bloomington, where he directed the production of table-model and car radios before leaving the company altogether in 1944 in order to create his own firm, Sarkes Tarzian Enterprises.

During the postwar era, as television began gaining momentum, Tarzian's company was heavily involved in some of the earliest trials in VHF audio broadcasting. He also continued to develop and manufacture equipment, including low-cost tuners and other components that were used by almost every television set maker in the country.

As business grew, a second plant in Pennsylvania was added, but Tarzian had his eye on another venture altogether. He wanted to create an entity that

The WTTV studios today at 3490 Bluff Road in Indianapolis, a shadow of the bustling building it once was. *Author's private collection.*

would serve to make his hometown and community a better place to live. The answer, he felt, was initially in a five-thousand-watt commercial radio station, WTTS, but it wasn't long before Tarzian was lured by the prospect of a Bloomington-based television station that could broadcast a variety of programs to be enjoyed by residents throughout the region.

Naturally, the idea was not without its detractors. Tarzian faced a number of naysayers who said that even wealthy stations were losing money hand over fist in an effort to stay afloat. What chance did he have with a small local operation? It was an expensive proposition, and well-meaning friends warned Tarzian that it wasn't likely he would ever find a talented enough staff locally to help him run the place. Even if he did, no local businessman would consider television for its advertising.

Thankfully, for Tarzian's sake, they were wrong on all accounts. Undeterred by the warnings, Tarzian pushed ahead. He used a vacant drugstore adjacent to his plant as a studio/transmitter building and found that he had no trouble rounding up a group of skilled and talented people to get the station off the ground. General Manager Bob Lemon, who had an accounting background and was well connected throughout the community, was one of the first employees, followed by Bob Petranoff, just out of Indiana University as the program director. Sue Bartlett, at the age of twenty-three, became the station's copy chief, and Norman Cissna was named sales manager of the new venture.

"Sarkes was a brilliant man, and I really admired him," said Brian (Jerry) Reynolds, a former Channel 4 employee who served as a studio assistant, director, writer, crew member, artist and puppet builder among his varied duties at the station. "He was unpretentious and very down-to-earth."

Reynolds said that the station used WATS lines that connected to different parts of the country on a variety of bandwidths, and on many occasions when he was working late, Tarzian would call in to find out who was on the line. He recalls:

> *It was usually the radio DJs who were using it to call their girlfriends in other parts of the world. WTTV sat on a huge parcel of land in Bloomington, with lots of deer, and the Tarzian mansion sat at the top of the hill. We were 150 yards away from the house at the original studio, but I never made it up that driveway to the big house. Today, the original studio has been torn down, and the property is a condo development, with the mansion serving as the clubhouse. Still, I have fond memories of Sarkes. He really understood his industry, and I was in awe of him.*

WTTV HITS THE AIRWAVES

WTTV went on the air on November 11, 1949, as only the second television station in the state of Indiana (WFBM, later known as WRTV was the first) and was originally broadcast via Channel 10 before making the move to Channel 4 in 1954. During those first seven years on the air, WTTV was a local affiliate for ABC, NBC and the DuMont networks but eventually became an independent station in 1956.

After declaring its independence, the team at WTTV moved their main studios to 3490 Bluff Road, on the south side of Indianapolis (keeping the Bloomington studio as a satellite station known as WTTK). The station signed on each afternoon at two o'clock, with original programming beginning at four o'clock, just in time for the after-school crowd and families who enjoyed their "new" TV dinners around the tube in the evening.

The WTTV-4 promotional patch given to viewers at local meet-and-greet events. *Courtesy of Peggy Powis.*

With the lack of a parent company supplying additional shows, WTTV earned its reputation as a station that aired local sporting competitions (Big Ten basketball being a favorite) as well as news casts, syndicated material such as old movies, cartoons and original low-budget shows. Talk shows included *Coffee with Carter*, *Mid-Morning with Barbara Stock* (later known for her work on *Spenser: For Hire*), *The Jim Gerard Show* and *The Billie Boucher Show*. "I was a personality, or 'talent,'" recalled Boucher, who served as WTTV's women's director in 1964. Her half-hour program offered Hoosier housewives a dose of facts, fashion and household hints, along with celebrity interviews and "special" guests, many of whom were members of the WTTV crew, including Bob Glaze. "I had forgotten that I sang on her show," said Bob Glaze. "I ran camera on her show, but I guess she was kind enough to let me sing on it…she was a dear lady."

Paul Ernst, another member of the production team, joined Glaze on a Simon and Garfunkle-esque rendition of "Shenandoah" during a broadcast highlighting their rich harmonies. "I had forgotten…he and I were a pretty good team," Glaze noted.

It was a period in television history when anything could happen. During the WTTV Channel 4 fiftieth anniversary special, Boucher remembered that in her six years at the station, she moved from community club awards director to account executive and women's director before moving on to WRTV Channel 6. "You could do just about anything," she said. "We sponsored the Miss Indiana pageant…I interviewed Dick Van Dyke and his brother Jerry…I even have a picture of me with Sharon Tate before she was taken from us. It was a fun time."

Early Children's Programming

In an effort to establish itself as a contender for the Indianapolis television market, WTTV green lighted and cancelled a number of kiddie shows throughout the 1950s and '60s. *Randy and Friends* was an early children's program that featured the puppet creations of Chuck Marlow, a man who not only had a side gig as Larry Chambers's straight man on the *Ruffles the Clown Show* but who also donned a clown suit for commercials in which he appeared.

The station's first hit children's show was *The Old Western Ledger*. Designed around a film presentation rather than a cartoon package, the show was hosted by station announcer "Uncle Bob" Hardy, who fell into the role accidentally when the original host's alcoholism prevented him from carrying out his duties. When Hardy became the permanent replacement, he created a full on-air persona, complete with traditional cowboy clothes and a golden palomino named Rhythm.

Hardy's show proved to be so successful that a fan club and endorsements followed. According to Hollis, H.P. Wasson and Company was curious as to whether the local personality could help boost its bottom line. The company booked Hardy and Little Rascals host Les Satherthwaite to appear at the department store, and within a single day, employees noted that over twenty thousand people descended on the fifth-floor toy department in order to attend the meet-and-greet. The lunch counter even created a special "Uncle Bob"–themed meal and served more than seven hundred of them. Needless to say, Wasson's quickly became a WTTV advertiser.

The next big children's personality to come out of the station was "Happy Herb the Sailor." Portrayed by a sailor suit–wearing Herb Issacs, the character debuted in 1959 after WTTV acquired a package of Popeye cartoons. "Herb was true to his name—a constantly upbeat, smiling, energetic seaman who led the audience through various comedic and educational segments between films," wrote Hollis.

An autograph card from the 1970s featuring Cowboy Bob, Sammy Terry and Janie.
These cards were mailed to viewers and given out at personal appearances. *Courtesy of Staci Edwards*.

With a winning formula now in place, other shows found their way to the WTTV lineup. Mary Ellen Reed, who had already appeared on several other shows, was asked to host her own cartoon program, and Betsy Goodspeed, who hosted a daily talk show, pre-empted her Wednesday timeslot to visit the *Magic House*, where she conversed with a group of puppets known as the Pop-Ups.

All Hands on Deck

Those who worked at WTTV throughout the 1960s, '70s and '80s recalled the "all hands on deck" mentality that permeated the station. A programming director might serve as an on-air personality or as a crewmember on another show. The advertising team and set designers also pitched in wherever needed in order to help the station offer something special to its viewers. One never knew where a job at WTTV might lead, but one thing was certain: if someone had a hidden talent, chances are that it wouldn't stay hidden very long.

Employees never knew what new break might be waiting around the corner or what iconic roles they would inspire. Little did they know that those characters would become household names and win them legions of fans from the young viewers who connected with them thanks to the magic of television and an independent station with plenty of vision. "We were the little station that could," recalls Glaze. "Everybody wore a lot of hats in those days. I was just among those who wore ones that allowed me to be on both sides of the camera."

CHAPTER 2

Pleasant Nightmares

In the dead of night, when the moon is high and the ill winds blow, and the banshees cry and the moonlight casts and unearthly glow; arise, my love, with tales of woe.
—*Sammy Terry introduction*

As a young man growing up in Decatur, Illinois, Bob Carter dreamed of becoming a professional musician. He was an avid drummer until a broken wrist derailed his plans at the age of twenty. Disappointed but undaunted, Carter gave up his passion for percussion, at least temporarily, and turned his attention to academics, graduating from Millikin University with a major in theater and radio. He later earned his master's degree in television production from Syracuse University and began his stint in broadcasting in Peoria, Illinois. Before long, Carter made his way to a Fort Wayne station owned by Tarzian, where he served as an announcer, director and producer before also landing gigs as an on-screen personality.

One of Carter's early duties at the station was filling in for the vacationing Dick Clark on the wildly popular dance program *American Bandstand*. According to Carter's son Mark, the weeklong stint prompted the station to develop its own rock-and-roll-based show and wanted Carter to host it. Originally called *Movietime 21*, the show was going to showcase fun movies that would appeal to the hipster set, but when that didn't catch on, they segued to their own *Bandstand*-esque show and called it *Club 21*.

Bob Carter posing for a *Movietime 21* publicity shot. The show never aired, being replaced by *Club 21*, an *American Bandstand*–style dance show in Fort Wayne. *Courtesy of SammyTerryNightmares.com.*

In addition to introducing songs and interviewing 1950s musical artists such as Bobby Rydell, Carter did live commercials between segments. It was during one such a segment that Carter unwittingly coined a phrase that went on to become a classic advertising slogan.

The sponsor was Kentucky Fried Chicken, and the commercial required Carter to snack on a drumstick and talk up the product prior to interviewing his next guest. Lacking a napkin with which to wipe his hands, Carter impulsively licked his fingers clean and pronounced the chicken "finger-lickin' good." Colonel Harland Sanders heard the comment, thought it was brilliant and asked if he could use it. Being friendly with the famous Indiana native and KFC entrepreneur, Carter gave him the slogan and never profited from the clever turn of phrase.

Eventually, Carter made his way to Indianapolis in order to take a position at WTTV, where his ability to multitask was once again put to good use. He not only produced and directed programs but also served as an on-air announcer for *Championship Wrestling*, worked with the advertising department and hosted a three-hour morning talk show called *Coffee with Carter*. "That show eventually became the *Bob Braun Show* and then the *Jim Gerard Show*," recalls Carter.

Originally shot live outside the studio or at a local shopping center, *Coffee with Carter* showcased man-on-the-street interviews and covered local events in a way that highlighted Carter's improvisational skills. He said that part of the fun was in not knowing who would happen by or in what direction the conversation would go. Every day was different, but he was always game to play straight man to anyone who came along.

In a newspaper article from the early 1960s, Carter recalled a young boy who convinced him to try out a seven-foot-tall homemade bicycle on the show. As he tooled around on the mechanism, the young man mentioned that he hadn't installed any brakes on it and didn't know how to get the rider down without breaking both of his ankles in the process.

On another occasion, an outdoor baby contest was delayed for several hours due to a sudden downpour. By the time the pageant got underway and the judging commenced, everyone was soaked, and nearly all of the 420 contestants had food smeared on them. "One of the women held her forty-five-pound child in her arms for three hours. I was amazed at the way everyone held their temper," Carter recalled of the pre-*Toddlers & Tiaras* era.

Coffee with Carter ultimately moved into the studio, giving Carter more control over the program's content and guests. Art Hook, Carter's programming director, said that the show's lengthy time slot might have

Bob Carter and an unknown man outside the WTTV-4 studios on Bluff Road. *Courtesy of Sammy Terry Nightmares.com.*

caused any other host to run for the hills, but Carter took it all in stride and filled the show with news and weather reports and cartoons and chatted with guests about anything and everything in order to fill up the time. "With Bob, I tell him three hours, and he says, 'How can I fit it all in?'" Hook said.

THE RISE OF SAMMY

Carter was content with his gig as a talk show host, engaging his guests about everything from hangnails to hat makers and A-bombs to apple crops, but in 1962, he created the character for which he would be best known: Indiana's legendary graveyard ghoul, Sammy Terry.

Movie studios with a cache of vintage horror flicks packaged their titles and sold them to independent stations throughout the country as inexpensive time fillers that required little more than a sponsor. It wasn't unheard of for local stations to coerce their weatherman, on-air announcer or whoever happened to be hanging around the studio into taking on the role of horror

An early publicity photo of WTTV-4's horror host Sammy Terry (aka Bob Carter) before the green makeup. *Courtesy of SammyTerryNightmares.com.*

host. Those who were game for the gig would don a Dracula cape, mad scientist lab coat or other creepy costume and create a scary-sounding name to complete the overall effect. Some monikers included Ghastly Ashley, the Cool Ghoul and, of course, Elvira, Mistress of the Dark.

Undaunted by the time constraints, the WTTV-4 crew swung into action in order to transform Carter into his new alter ego. The wife of one of the sales reps sewed the original cowl for him, which he paired with a black windbreaker that he wore backward. A large coffee table became the central set decoration, along with a broken rooster lamp and a fake window frame adorning the background. With only four days left to go, all that was missing was a name. The character required something creepy but not corny. The group finally settled on Sammy Terry due to the fact that when pronounced quickly, it became a play on the word "cemetery." A day before going on the air, Hook, who had some experience with stage makeup, gave Carter's face a sallow, gaunt look that would appear menacing on camera. "But we still didn't have a script," Carter noted.

Luckily for Carter, the first movie scheduled to air was *The Mummy* (1932), starring Boris Karloff. It was one of his favorite films, and he knew the storyline well enough to improvise an introduction. But creating the dialogue for the commercial spots that ushered in the sponsor's products was another matter entirely. Carter said that for the first several months *Shock Theater* was on the air, he sat on the floor with his legs under the coffee table for the weekly film introduction, and while the audience at home watched the latest tale of terror, he and the crew at the station sat around mapping out what he would say and do next. "Three months later…we had a written script and cue cards, but up until then, it was strictly ad-lib—literally off the seat of my pants sitting on the floor," he recalled. "I can't remember how long it was before we got a coffin and a set."

One of Bob Glaze's first responsibilities at WTTV-4 was operating the scoop light on the *Sammy Terry Show* during the era when it was still shot in black-and-white. Glaze said that there was something about the eeriness of those grainy days that allowed the theater of the mind to take over and terrify the viewers at home. Glaze's job was to follow Carter around on the floor with the light that would give Sammy Terry his ghoulish appearance. He said that although his jeans were usually filthy by the time the show was over, he was proud to be part of the show as a crew member, producer or acting the part of Sammy's rocking chair.

"I enjoyed working with Bob; he was a jack of all trades," Glaze said. "The irony is that he was such a Christian person, but he could do this character so convincingly! He would write the most delightful scripts, and we would bite our tongues laughing."

After the initial thirteen-week run of the new show, the original sponsor went out of business, but there was another advertiser in line ready to continue the Friday night fright fest. Carter said it was the first clue he had that Sammy Terry was no flash in the pan. "It was the longest thirteen-week contract in history. I was on the air thirty years!" Carter said.

In the three decades that *Shock Theater* and its subsequent incarnations (*Nightmare Theater* and *Sammy Terry*) graced the Friday night time slot, it was a must-see for fans, who curled into a corner of their sofa in time to see Sammy rise from his coffin in his cozy dungeon and offer a hearty "Good evening" before waxing poetically about the things that go bump in the night.

There are all kinds of weird and unsavory monsters in the world—animalistic beasts, vampires, werewolves, gorillas, vipers and, of course, politicians—but now, with technology and the exploration of space, a new

Artwork for the original Sammy Terry show, *Nightmare Theater*, on WTTV-4, circa 1964. *Courtesy of SammyTerryNightmares.com.*

> *terror has appeared to traumatize you into a hysterical passion. For after my tale of terror tonight, you will be ready to scream at the top of your lungs!*
> —*Sammy Terry on* Die, Monster, Die!, *October 1985*

The movies were typical B-level fare, and few could be considered high art. Some of Sammy's offerings included *The Creature from the Black Lagoon* (1954), *The Horror of Party Beach* (1964) and *And Now the Screaming Starts* (1973), starring Stephanie Beacham, Ian Olgivy and legendary British actor Peter Cushing. But it wasn't the films that kept viewers tuning in; it was the character that Carter created that the fans appreciated. "In between features, Sammy Terry would discuss the movies, make jokes with George the Spider and other regulars (Ghost Girl, Ghoulsbie), have an occasional guest, talk about the Pacers, or show off the Crayola drawings…that local children would send to WTTV," wrote longtime Sammy Terry fan Alfred Eaker. "Sammy had an inimitable laugh that would send shivers down the eight-year-old spine. If you made it to the end of the night, Sammy would

Left: Sammy Terry quickly became the city's favorite ghoul as he rose from his coffin every Friday night on WTTV-4. *Courtesy of SammyTerryNightmares.com.*

Below: Mary Ellen Reed, who played Wilhelmina, Sammy Terry's housekeeper, gets into her car after a day of taping. She later went on to host *Lunchtime Theater*, WTTV-4's midday cartoon show. *Courtesy of SammyTerryNightmares.com.*

retreat to his coffin and bestow his wish of 'Many Pleasant Nightmares.' You knew with excitement and dread that he would return the following Friday."

Frank Fettinger posted his Sammy Terry memories on E-gors Chamber of TV Horror Hosts website, saying that like many others, he had a fondness for *Nightmare Theater*:

> *My brother and I, being youngsters who got up for school early everyday, had a hard time staying up too late on the weekend, and making it through the whole Sammy Terry double feature was a goal we strived for, and fell short of, every Friday night. We grew up with Sammy, and as the years went by, the realism and the scariness of his sets and his looks were replaced by an appreciation for the campiness of it all and an understanding of some of his wry humor.*

Indianapolis paranormal historian Alan E. Hunter began watching Sammy Terry in the late 1960s during Friday night sleepovers with his pals from Lew Wallace School #107. Hunter said that he loved the campy atmosphere Carter created with his ghoulish persona before the National Anthem played and the station signed off for the night. Rubber spiders, rubber dishwashing gloves with veins drawn on them and a cheap plywood coffin should not have been scary, and yet somehow it was. "The props were stored in a shed behind the studios," he recalled. "I had an uncle who worked there, and he let us in several times to see them. When WTTV was sold, I understood that several 'treasures' were thrown into the dumpsters… but a few employees squirreled away some things for themselves."

In 1983, Fettinger attended a Sammy Terry appearance in Washington, Indiana. "I think we were the only eighteen-, twenty- and forty-year-olds in attendance that day," he said. "There was an autograph session in the lobby, and I will never forget standing head and shoulders above a sea of kids that surrounded me, trying to get to the table where Sammy sat, signing posters of himself. I still have that autographed poster."

Like Fettinger, Hunter got to meet Carter in character a few times when he made appearances around Indianapolis during his heyday. During a church lock-in in Avon, Hunter was a five-year-old participant when Carter arrived to do a live radio remote as Sammy and invited Hunter onstage with him. "He scared me so badly that I literally wet myself. Thankfully, there are no pictures of that."

Despite his fear of Sammy Terry, Hunter cherishes the memories of hobnobbing with local celebrities and favorite children's hosts who were so

In the 1970s, Sammy Terry's set became more elaborate and looked like a stone dungeon. *Courtesy of SammyTerryNightmares.com.*

accessible in those days. "They were people who lived in the communities, shopped in the local stores, could be found substitute teaching in your school, or a member of your church community. It's sad that today's kids do not have the same experiences that we did. Kids need those kinds of celebrities in their lives."

SEPARATE LIVES

In the Carter household, Sammy Terry was like another member of the family—a high-profile persona that was patiently tolerated by one and all. Carter's son Mark recalled that many times, family dinners at a local restaurant were interrupted by Sammy's well-meaning fans, eager to meet the man behind the makeup. He said that his father was always very appreciative of the public's affection and never hesitated to sign an autograph or pose for a picture.

Mark understood the interest in his father's alter ego. From seventh grade through high school, Mark had made regular appearances on the program as Ghoulsbie and attended many meet-and-greets along the way. Whenever he was scheduled to tape his segment, Mark's mother would allow him to leave school early in order to get down to the WTTV studios. Looking back on the experience, he realized how lucky he was to be part of the show at such a young age, and he has great appreciation for how special a time it was. "Sammy meant so much to so many people over the years, and he continues to evoke a feeling of nostalgia in those who remember their Friday nights with him," Mark said.

But that did not mean that Mark watched *Nightmare Theater* every Friday night. A strict bedtime of ten o'clock prevented him from watching the show he appeared on. It wasn't until he was in eighth grade (and had been on the show for a year) that he was able to see the show that made his father so famous.

In 1972, Sammy celebrated his tenth anniversary on the air with a very special presentation of *Nightmare Theater* that featured an introduction by the Master of Macabre, Vincent Price. Guest host John Stanley ushered in a cavalcade of well-wishers who wanted to give Sammy their regards between segments of *The Ghost of Frankenstein*. The show included appearances by WRTV-6 personality Harlow Hickenloper (aka Hal Fryer), WISH-8's Mike Ahern, "Cowboy" Bob Glaze, Sally Jo Fridley of the Sally Jo and Friends show, Cincinnati's "Cool Ghoul," the Ben Davis High School Marching Band and Sid Collins, "Voice of the Indianapolis 500," who presented Sammy with a painting that had been displayed at the Children's Museum Guild's Haunted House. Legendary wrestler "Dick the Bruiser" phoned in to say hello, while representatives from local government officials arrived with honors for Sammy. Indianapolis mayor Richard Lugar cited Sammy's contributions to the city, as well as his service in making the community a better place. The Marion County sheriff's department sent a representative to make the ghoul an honorary deputy, and Peggy Campbell, press secretary for then-governor Edgar D. Whitcomb, bestowed a proclamation that read:

Whereas, Sammy Terry, the terribly horrifying host of the weekly, scary, nail-biting program Nightmare Theater on WTTV Channel 4 arises from the dead to celebrate this eventful day, which happens to be his tenth anniversary on the air and also his birthday, and whereas the dead-ridden figure of Sammy Terry will diminish even further in that he has aged one more horrible year, and whereas our ghastly Friday night entertainer grasps

Mark Carter, son of Bob Carter, made several appearances on *Nightmare Theater* as Ghoulsbie. Today, he has assumed the role of Sammy Terry and continues to terrify and delight the community. *Courtesy of SammyTerryNightmares.com.*

his audience with his bellowing ghoulish laughter that echoes throughout the viewer's home, and whereas when the other ghosts, goblins and witches, all of whom are his friends, arise on Halloween night, so will Sammy Terry, who is more frightening than all of the goblins put together. And now, therefore, I, Edgar D. Whitcomb, governor of the State of Indiana, proclaim that as the moon creeps over the horizon on October 31, 1972, it will be Sammy Terry Day throughout the State of Indiana, and I urge fellow Hoosier citizens to recognize this memorable day by being sad.

The success of his television persona ultimately enabled Carter to resuscitate a dream that was gone but not forgotten—his passion for music. Later that year, Carter opened the Family Music Center on North Shadeland Avenue, a store that specialized in a variety of instruments, music lessons and one of the best collections of sheet music in Indianapolis. Carter still appeared as Sammy on the small screen and made countless personal appearances, but the store afforded him the chance to separate somewhat from his iconic role and focus on another interest. Ironically, few patrons who frequented the store for the first time made the connection between the man behind the counter and the host of the *Sammy Terry Show*. "I don't recall ever seeing Sammy out of costume unless it was at his music store in Lawrence, and I'm not sure I identified him with his TV persona at the time," said Matt Hodge.

Carter was fine with that. In fact, he relished in the anonymity the store gave him, because he knew that if he deliberately drew attention to his television character, customers would focus more on ghouls than the guitars, band instruments or piano arrangements they came in to buy. Of course, it wasn't always possible to keep everyone in the dark. Every once in a while, especially when a hint of that eerie, ghoulish laugh seeped out, an unsuspecting customer would discover his secret identity. "I've always kept the two [lives] separate," Carter said in an *Indianapolis Star* interview. "Otherwise, I would spend the whole time shaking hands, signing autographs and laughing that laugh."

The truth about Carter's Sammy Terry connection was even hidden from his employees, who often found out on their own. Several were surprised to learn that they were working for a legend, as Carter was about as far from his television personality as one can get. When Carter closed the store after twenty-nine years at the age of seventy-one, most of his customers and employees looked back on the man who loved music rather than the local horror host. "No matter where I go from here on, I will never meet anyone better to work for—bar none," said Jeff Ehlert, who worked at the Family Music Center for more than three years. He admitted that as much as he loved working for Carter, he was also a Sammy fan. "That was a Friday night ritual for me."

KEEPING THE LEGACY ALIVE

Carter remained modest about the legendary role he created that seemed to resonate with a lot of viewers. When the last episode of the *Sammy Terry Show* aired in 1989 and the Family Music Center closed in July 2001, Carter made no plans to retire his cowl. He continued to make local appearances in Fountain Square or other locales during Halloween, though he no longer performed at children's birthday parties. He always had a great turnout, and the fans still loved to see their beloved ghoul.

In 2003, WTTV-4 asked Sammy to return to the small screen once again for a two-hour Halloween special entitled *Sammy Terry's Scary Tales*. Using the classic intro to the *Sammy Terry Show*, Sammy shared stories of local haunts featured in Wanda Lou Willis's book *Hoosier Haunted Trails*, complete with reenactments of events filmed in the original ghostly location. One of the stories, "100 Steps," is a tale in which the foolhardy, with the help of a ghostly caretaker, climb to the top of the steps in order to find the age at which they will die. Others report being shoved down the stairs by the unseen caretaker if they forget to count the steps along their journey.

Sammy did not disappoint his fans, who were eager to celebrate his return on "Sammy Terry's Scary Tales." The show was well received, and more installments were ordered. On October 30, 2004, Sammy hosted the classic horror film *The Terror* and shared more of his "scary tales" with his audience.

During the Horror Hounds convention in downtown Indianapolis one year, Sammy Terry made a special guest appearance. Much to the surprise of several attendees, the crowds flocked away from many of the more established stars on scene, which included Syd Haag, Bill Mosley and Tom Savini. Rusty Ammerman, a Connersville native, was on hand for the event and said that he was a fan of Sammy Terry in addition to Cincinnati's "Cool Ghoul" (played by Dick Von Hoene), who appeared on channel WXIX. He said that the Cool Ghoul was more whimsical than Sammy, with his

Hal Fryer (aka Harlow Hickenlopper, a longtime kiddie host on WRTV-6) stopped by the set of Sammy Terry's *Scary Tales* in the early 2000s. *Courtesy of SammyTerryNightmares.com.*

tongue-fluttering trill, but that Sammy was considerably more sinister than his counterpart. "When it was announced that Sammy Terry would be on the floor for the next hour, it was crazy to watch people walk away from these truly famous people," said Rusty Ammerman, "They were all asking, 'What's a Sammy Terry?' I found myself explaining that he was kind of like the local version of Elvira. Luckily, all of them had a similar kind of horror host in their own hometowns, so they totally got it." Mark Carter recalls, "Linda Blair of *The Exorcist* even came up to my father because she had to meet the guy who had created such a fuss. It was a special event, and he was happy to be part of it."

Sammy Terry mugs with a young fan at the Children's Museum of Indianapolis in 2012. *Author's private collection.*

In time, health issues convinced Carter that he was no longer up to the task of being Sammy. Though Mark and the rest of the Carter family were sure the character would begin and end with Bob, Carter realized that Sammy needed to live on, and it was time to pass the coffin to a new generation. He bequeathed the entire Sammy Terry enterprise to his son Mark and encouraged him to keep the legacy alive. While Mark Carter originally planned on continuing his role as the "Son of Sammy," Bob championed the idea that there was only one Sammy Terry, and now it was Mark. "It felt very natural for me to become Sammy," said Mark, noting that his father and he are similar in many ways, including their approach to the Sammy character. "Of course I knew the shoes I was to fill were huge, and there was a question as to whether or not the character would be adopted by the public and if Sammy would once again have staying power. You always wonder if people will accept it and if the legacy will live on, because sometimes it doesn't."

But Mark Carter did not have to worry. Fans of Sammy were only too happy to see their favorite horror host return, and they have been extremely kind with their feedback, most of which centers around the uncanny similarity between Mark and his father. Mark said that being Bob's son has certainly helped people give him a chance, but most fans have said that seeing Mark in the cowl allows them to relive a little portion of their childhood. "Sammy continues to evolve, but he's never so scary that he really frightens you. It's a fun scare that lets you play with your fears a little," Mark said, mentioning that the theater of the mind tends to be more horrifying than anything a special-effects department can come up with. Though he knows that Sammy has to remain current to connect with the current generation, he doesn't try to stray too far from the established path. "We're picking up right where Dad left off," he said. "The Sammy of the 1960s is different than he was in the '70s and '80s."

Mark still films occasional Sammy Terry shows for WTTV-4 on Halloween night and at various other times throughout the year. He uses set pieces from the original Nightmare Theater and is constantly working to make sure that his interpretation of the character is dead-on and exact. "The shows take about six hours to film, and then I rely on the editing and production talents of Brett Pittman to pull it all together," Mark said during a recent photo shoot on the Sammy Terry set.

And what does the original ghoul think of the new and even more "horrible" Sammy? Actually, he couldn't be happier, according to Mark. Carter, who is resting comfortably in a nursing home, enjoys the feedback Sammy has received for his sold-out stage shows, his meet-and-greets and his

Young Sammy Terry fans gang up on their favorite ghoul at the Children's Museum of Indianapolis Halloween celebration in 2012. *Author's private collection.*

occasional television specials. "We did a real throwback Sammy Terry stage show recently in Muncie that sold out very quickly," said Mark. "There were six hundred people there, and it was like one of those old-style vaudeville shows, with plenty of spooky stuff that isn't terribly scary but is a lot of fun to watch."

WTTV has also allowed Mark to don the Sammy gear and load digital shorts on their website in which he offers soliloquies similar to his father's. Though it is all-new material written by Mark, it is 100 percent Sammy Terry. While there have been hopes that the *Sammy Terry Show* will be resurrected in its old Friday night timeslot, at the moment, fans will have to be content with the occasional special, as the station cannot commit to a weekly show at the present time. However, fans can always find Sammy on his personal website and on social media sites such as Facebook. Mark said that he often shares the e-mails and feedback he gets from Sammy's fans with his father whenever he can. "He doesn't really understand what Facebook is, but he knows it's out there and that he has tens of thousands of fans online," said Mark, marking Sammy's fiftieth anniversary at a Children's Museum event

Sammy Terry's dungeon portrait created by Pat Flanagan is a set piece that is familiar to fans of the show. *Courtesy of SammyTerryNightmares.com.*

in 2012. "I used to bring him all of the comments, but now there are so many that it's overwhelming. Still, he enjoys knowing that people are still responsive to that character that he created out of desperation…it was only supposed to be on the air thirteen weeks, but it still lives on."

In 2012, Sammy Terry was inducted into the Horror Host Hall of Fame as the longest-running horror host of all time, and Mark Carter plans on continuing the Sammy Terry legacy as long as he is able, because for him, it is a labor of love. "The best thing about being Sammy Terry is listening to the stories of the fans. It's an honor to play a character that has such an impact and to preserve those memories for generations. Even though we are bringing Sammy to a whole new generation of viewers, we won't divert too much from what people know and love."

CHAPTER 3

Music Teacher Hits the Right Note

Of course I feel good!
—*the* Janie *show, circa 1980*

Though Sammy Terry was a big hit with viewers of all ages, the king of central Indiana's undead was not a "kiddie host" in the traditional sense. The personality dominating that market was "Happy Herb the Sailor," who showcased Popeye cartoons on his afternoon show. In 1963, the station made a change in personnel and hired a young music teacher who came with plenty of broadcast experience, a warm, engaging smile and a natural ease in front of the camera that made her a staple in homes for more than two decades. Her name was Janie.

Born in northern Indiana, the girl who would become Janie Hodge moved with her family to Indianapolis when she was in the fourth grade. An only child and a natural go-getter, she began taking dance and music lessons at a young age and later became an entrepreneur when she mailed away for a box of greeting cards from an ad she saw in the back of a comic book and began selling her wares door-to-door in her neighborhood and around her grandmother's house in Worthington. "I made a lot of money," Janie said. "I was a very good salesman. After that, I worked my way through college selling clothing at a department store whenever I was home for the weekend or on summer vacation."

Hodge attended Shortridge High School, where she participated in a variety of extracurricular activities ranging from the newspaper to plays, debate club and chorus before majoring in music education at Indiana University. Her first position in the classroom was, ironically, in front of the television cameras. In 1960, Hodge was hired by the Ford Foundation to teach closed-circuit music to first, second and third graders in schools throughout Hagerstown, Maryland. It was a novel approach before the advent of online classes. Students watched each lesson while their teacher monitored the class and took notes on their progress, letting Hodge know when concepts needed to be repeated or reviewed. "It was an innovative experiment to see what classes could be taught successfully [through the television medium] and at what level," Hodge said.

A New Miss Nancy

After two years with the Ford program, Hodge traveled to Baltimore to audition for Bert Claster, who along with his wife Nancy created *Romper Room* in 1954. There was a temporary position available in Milwaukee filling in for a teacher/hostess who was on medical leave. "A friend of mine suggested that I audition for it, and it occurred to me that it wasn't that big of a leap from the kind of thing I was already doing," she said.

Romper Room was an education-based program designed to entertain the preschool set. The show was sold to every major market in the country, whether a station bought the syndicated version (using Baltimore's hostess) or a franchised version, in which scripts were sent and a local personality became the classroom teacher. On each half-hour episode, the teacher spent the time reading to the "class" (usually about seven or eight children) on the set and helping them learn their alphabet, manners and values with gentleness and patience. "It was like the old Kindergarten College that we used to have around here," Hodge said.

Hodge won the audition and took the six-month position but found the Wisconsin winters hard to get used to. She began looking for a job in a warmer climate and was pleased to learn that there was a job opening at WTTV in Indianapolis. While visiting her family over Mother's Day, she interviewed at the station and was hired to take over the afternoon cartoon show in the 4:00–6:00 p.m. time slot. "I had the distinction of being hired by two different stations that same weekend," Hodge explained. "I was hired by Channel 8 to host the women's program for the summer, and then we started *Popeye and Janie* in the fall at Channel 4."

Norm Roberts and Janie Hodge discuss her show at the WTTV-4 studios in the 1960s. *Courtesy of Brian (Jerry) Reynolds.*

A piece of loose-leaf notebook paper highlights the history of Hodge's tenure on television. *Popeye and Janie* (later known as *Janie's Treehouse*) debuted on WTTV in August 1963 from the radio building within the Indiana State Fairgrounds. The set featured the letter "J," live guests and kids. From 4:30 to 6:00 p.m., Hodge offered the cartoon package and would sing songs such as "If You're Happy and You Know It." She would tell jokes, read mail, show pictures sent in by viewers and choose prizes for whatever giveaway the station's sponsors happened to be promoting at the time. She said the small studios and large equipment made for a tight squeeze in the space, but she was happy to have the creative license to build her show from the ground up. Like Sammy Terry's show, there was no format for the live, black-and-white show. As a teacher, she was determined to have some educational components in the program, but she realized that after a full day of learning, kids were ready to be entertained by their favorite cartoon characters and not in the mood for another lesson.

Eschewing traditional curriculum, Hodge asked artists to stop by and explain their techniques and invited professionals from the Indianapolis Zoo to bring in exotic animals and explain their unique characteristics. She knew she could sneak in a little knowledge here and there, provided that it wasn't blatantly educational. She also learned that in addition to the children tuning in, adults who worked in local factories and were home from the first shift often turned on the show to watch cartoons and relax after a hard day's work. "It didn't hurt that I wore short skirts and looked good," she added.

In addition to appearing on camera, Hodge made personal appearances at Burger Chef Restaurants, Crossroads Carnivals (which raised money for Crossroads Rehabilitation Center) and Pepsi parties held at a viewer's home. "Whenever someone won a Pepsi party, they were allowed to invite ten friends to come over, and I would come in with one of the guys to do a little show. We would then have Pepsi or popcorn or Chesty potato chips, which were another sponsor at the time," she said.

A Janie appearance always drew a good-size crowd, thanks to her show's popularity and appeal. However, when she visited smaller towns to ride in a parade or stop by a Burger Chef Restaurant, she said the lines would stretch down the street, as fans hoped to get an autograph, take a picture or just say hello.

And when she wasn't serving as the queen of cartoons, Hodge supplemented her income by working as a teacher in the Indianapolis Public Schools. She said when the last bell rang, she jumped in her car and raced to the studio in order to be on time for the show. After the show, she would drive back to her Northside home in hopes of having dinner with her family. "Looking back, I wonder how I had that kind of energy," she laughed. "I did hire a teenager from North Central's home economics department to help prepare our meals though, so that helped."

JANIE MOVES TO MORNINGS

After the birth of her second child in 1972, Hodge's show moved to the mornings and adopted the simpler title of *Janie*. Station manager Don Tillman asked then nineteen-year-old Jerry Reynolds to take the helm of the new production. "Unlike some of the other Channel 4 personalities who I got to know as people first, Janie was a star to me because I watched her for years.

I was chomping at the bit to do the show, but I was nervous too. To me, there was no distinction between someone like Janie and Lucille Ball," he said.

Reynolds had built Rolly Bear, a puppet for the *Janie's Treehouse* show, in the afternoon and wrote an un-aired Cowboy Bob and Janie Christmas special, but he knew the opportunity to build Janie's new formatted show was the opportunity of a lifetime for a young college student.

From 7:00 to 9:00 a.m. each morning, Janie brought viewers the latest adventures of Hanna-Barbera favorites Snagglepuss and Yogi Bear. Unlike the original show, this incarnation was taped, unless a live remote was scheduled. This gave her a little more control over what happened on the air.

Hodge knew that live shows involved live problems, even for a professional such as herself. Fan letters were rarely screened for appropriateness before being read on the air, and in one such case, a letter supposedly written by a child was read one day, with Hodge carefully pronouncing the phonetically spelled words only to learn that they came out quite differently when spoken. "It was from some ornery person, and I read it live without knowing," Hodge said. "My whole crew was on the floor in hysterics. I didn't even know what I'd said. It went right over my head."

There was also the time when a live lion was brought into the studio, which made Hodge very nervous. The handler assured Hodge that the lion was trained, but she didn't trust it. She chose to interview the handler first and then hide behind the curtain when the lion was brought on the set after a commercial break. A member of her crew filled in to introduce the lion to the viewers and made small talk with the trainer. "The lion decided that he'd had enough, and he took off, with the owner on his knees being pulled across the studio. The lion whipped out his paw, knocked over a cameraman and went out the back door. I'm glad it wasn't me," she said.

But uncomfortable events still occurred, even with the best-laid plans. When Ringling Bros. and Barnum & Bailey Circus came to town, Hodge was part of the circus parade, leading from the west end of downtown Indianapolis to Market Square Arena. Afraid of animals, she was horrified to learn that she was expected to ride atop an elephant on the journey. "The hair on them is very wiry, and it hurt my legs. I was very uncomfortable," she said. "One of the drivers from the Indianapolis 500 was on an elephant next to me, and he said, 'Don't worry Janie, I'm scared too!' Finally, I started to cry, and one of my false eyelashes fell off…they got me off the elephant, so there was one rider-less animal in the parade."

Due to WTTV's partnership with local entities such as the Children's Museum, Hodge often taped segments at the venues, including the opening of the Indianapolis Zoo at Washington Park. She said Bud Hook, owner of Hook's Drug Stores, bought a buffalo for the zoo, and while she was conducting her interview, the buffalo, which was grazing on nearby grass, sneezed. "It got all over me," she said.

Queen of Cartoons

At the height of her television career, the *Janie* show periodically beat NBC's *Today Show* in local ratings. It was seen not only in Indiana but also in Ohio, Illinois and West Virginia. Hodge also played host to numerous guests—not only the folks who represented local organizations but also national television personalities such as Bob "Captain Kangaroo" Keeshan. Hodge said she was lucky to be included in anything that was going on around town, whether it was the circus or an event such as the Marion County Fair or Indiana State Fair (which allowed her to do live remotes). The Indianapolis Symphony invited her to participate in their children's concerts narrating "Peter and the Wolf." During the grand opening gala of Clowes Memorial Hall on the campus of Butler University, Hodge made a glamorous appearance, wearing a borrowed gown and the fanciest shoes she'd ever worn while interviewing attendees on the red carpet. "I still have them [the shoes]," she laughed in an interview. But she said that her biggest honor was interviewing First Lady Betty Ford when she was in town for an event at the Children's Museum. "Some of the newspaper people didn't even get to do that, so I was very thrilled," Hodge said.

Hodge said that there was no real secret to her success; it was merely looking into the camera and helping every viewer feel as though she was personally talking to him or her. Reynolds said it was a rare gift that he did not see in every performer. "She can look into the television camera and make you think she's talking right to you," he said. "She was really able to make that connection with her viewers."

Janie's morning show consisted of the same elements that viewers knew and loved from the afternoon but also contained a number of new puppet friends to serve as sidekicks for the host. According to the original art card Reynolds made for a pink, mop-headed monster: "Treble Clef lives in Janie's piano. He is the temperamental artist type. He can sing in any voice and will often sing to or with Janie. He is a cranky and suspicious type who doesn't trust anyone except Janie." "I did the original raspy voice of Treble Clef, but

The original artwork for Treble Clef, Janie's grouchy piano-dwelling monster who often sang with the popular hostess in his trademark raspy voice. *Courtesy of Brian (Jerry) Reynolds.*

An original art concept for Alf-A-Bet, a typical, absent-minded professor type who does all of the research on the Janie show and rarely stops talking once he gets started. *Courtesy of Brian (Jerry) Reynolds.*

Janie poses with her puppet pals at the piano on the set of the *Janie* show. *Courtesy of Brian (Jerry) Reynolds.*

Gilroy Gopher, Treble Clef and Janie's other sidekicks pose with their hostess for a *Janie* show publicity shot. *Courtesy of Brian (Jerry) Reynolds.*

the voice was done by several people over the years, including one guy who was a singer and thought it would destroy his vocal chords," Reynolds said. "Most of the other voices were not that far out, and even if the puppeteer changed over the years, the voice stayed relatively the same."

Reynolds said he felt a kinship to all of the characters on the show, which over time developed distinct personalities. Gilroy Gopher was the naïve Elmo-type innocent who represented the kids at home and served as a perfect foil to the ornery Treble Clef. Alf-A-Bet was the know-it-all but lasted only a year before being replaced by Professor IQ, the absent-minded professor.

Not only did Reynolds create the cast of Janie's show, write the dialogue and direct the production, but he also had a hand in building the sets, cobbling recycled materials to create an iconic world for thousands of fans throughout central Indiana. "We went to a second-hand store and found an old mailbox for Mailboxer, and Dick Blair and I bought piano keys to create the prop for Treble Clef's home. It worked out really well," he said.

NOT LIKE OTHER MOMS

Janie's son Matt, who was born the year her show moved to the mornings, said that the *Janie* set was a magical one. It was a colorful room with a door through which guests could enter and see the hollowed upright piano where Treble Clef lived alongside his frequent visitor Silly Snake. In the center of the room, there was a box that served as the seat for Gilroy Gopher, who was always ready for a chat with Janie, and on the other side of the set was a mail box (appropriately named Mailboxer) that, when opened, revealed a lone white glove that delivered the letters and jokes sent in by viewers. "Thinking of Mailboxer now makes me realize how creative the cast and crew of the show really were," Matt noted. "This puppet was nothing more than a hand inside a workman's glove inserted through a mailbox with the back cut out! It was economically brilliant and very entertaining. Who knew a glove could have so much personality?"

Although the television audience (and members of the production crew) regarded Janie as a major celebrity, for Matt and his older brother David, Janie was simply Mom. It wasn't until after he saw long lines of fans waiting patiently to meet his mother in order to get an autograph and take a picture that he understood that Janie wasn't like other mothers. Matt recalls:

> At home, she was mom, but then we would go out, and at some point, it hit me that everyone in the state seemed to know her. Looking back on it, I don't know how she did it all as well as she did. She was very nontraditional for that time, and I'm sure I took it for granted. But she's always been energetic and enthusiastic, giving her all to anything she was involved in.

Matt often accompanied his mother to the studio during the weekend tapings, exploring every inch of the station. He often ran through the reception area, past the front offices and down the hallway that led to the main filming studio. The standard "On Air" signal light in front of the door that led to the studio quickly became his first lesson in studio etiquette—when the red light is on, **DO NOT OPEN THIS DOOR!** "When that was the case, I would go around the studio to the break room and get a snack or go up the back hallway to the prop room that housed many strange objects from years past," Matt recalled.

In addition to playing with the original tombstones from Sammy Terry's show or the fence posts of *Chuckwagon Theater*, Matt would also explore the studio area (when the red light wasn't illuminated, of course). It was a world

Janie's son Matt became a regular fixture on his mother's show, often demonstrating crafts and hosting how-to segments. *Courtesy of Janie and Matt Hodge.*

of unlimited television magic, and he ran around the Jim Gerard talk show set and Sammy Terry's dungeon, adorned with its stone castle walls, fake cobwebs and, of course, the infamous coffin. The *Cowboy Bob's Corral* set and, of course, the set in which his mother worked were also areas of adventure.

According to Matt, the atmosphere on the set during a taping was extremely professional and straightforward. Janie arrived at the studio on Sunday morning to record all five shows that would be broadcasted during the week. The shows were recorded in order and in their entirety, with Hodge announcing her viewers' birthdays, introducing cartoon shorts, interacting with her puppets or interviewing a special guest.

One of Matt's favorite guests was a circus clown who came on set and gave Janie an extreme clown makeover. Viewers at home were able to watch the transformation process in seconds via fast forward photography, which offered the audience a glimpse of behind-the-scenes magic. "All of these extra segments were filmed in advance and then edited in at the appropriate time of the month," he said. "The bright lights would shine, the cameras would roll, Janie's smile would come to life and the crew acted like a well-oiled machine."

When one program was completed, Janie would change her costume (chosen from her personal wardrobe), the crew would set up for the next day of shooting and the process would continue until all five shows were complete and ready for broadcast. Matt recalls:

> *I do remember my mother working on her scripts at night and going to the library to gather visual material that provided inspiration for unique segments. She would spend time in her room with her felt-tipped pen and a yellow legal pad, jotting down ideas and rearranging different bits. I know it was a long and arduous process, but my mother always made it look effortless. The end result was always a well-polished product.*

When he was seven or eight years old, Matt followed his mother onto the small screen. As an imaginative and boisterous child, Janie bought him a thick book full of rainy-day projects to keep him busy. As Matt worked through each craft outlined in the book, he ultimately decided that the *Janie* show lacked a crafts segment, and he was determined to do something about it. He pitched the idea to his mother. "I had to sell Janie on the idea that her viewers would enjoy seeing a kid doing something they too could try at home," he recalled. "She loved the idea, but she didn't just give me the segment. I had to prove that I could do it. We called it 'Matt's Make-It Shop,' and it was on the air for about six or seven months. I even got fan mail!"

THE BEST IT COULD BE

As her show grew and evolved, Janie strove to make it the best it could be. Technology had evolved well enough to afford her the opportunity to use a blue screen in order to take her viewers on a fantasy journey to Europe, across the Grand Canyon or in a hot-air balloon. "My crew was always willing to work out my ideas and figure out how to implement them into the show," she said.

On set, there was also a board upon which Hodge posted the letters and pictures sent in by her viewers. As she went to commercial break, the camera would pan across the board so that her viewers could see the items they sent. It made them feel like they were a part of the show, but before long, there was

An early 1970s autograph card signed by Janie, Cowboy Bob and Peggy. These cards were mailed to fans and distributed at meet-and-greets. *Courtesy of Peggy Powis.*

a tremendous push to have groups of kids visit the set and be interviewed by Hodge, a move she was not inclined to make. It wasn't that she didn't want to see the kids; she didn't like the thought of inviting them behind her magic curtain and into her world of imagination. "Once you have children on the show, it limits what you're able to do," she said. Still, the requests kept coming, and she finally acquiesced. "I said we could do it two days a week, and the next thing you know, we had a two-year waiting period," Hodge said. "Finally, we changed it to having kids on every day. There were just so many who wanted to be on the show…to say their names and tell their jokes." Many of those former guests still remember their time on the air with fondness. "When I was a Campfire Girl in Noblesville, our group was on her show," said Regina Mack. "We also got to see Cowboy Bob!"

UNDISCOVERED TALENT

While on the air, Hodge never hesitated to ask members of her crew to join her in song and/or dance in front of the camera. Some were reluctant, but others, such as Bob Glaze, who was part of the production team, were always game to have fun in front of the camera. One day, while tuning Hodge's ukulele, Glaze mentioned that he had his guitar with him. Immediately, Hodge asked him to join her on set, and the two sang for the viewers. There was a natural chemistry between the two, and it wasn't long before Glaze became a regular on her show. "To this day, there are people who ask me if I am related to Janie," laughed Glaze. "We were never married, but I was on her show once a week or so."

The partnership led to the duo recording a Christmas album, which was rehearsed in Hodge's home after her family went to sleep. The album contained five traditional arrangements, including "Silent Night," "First Noel" and "It Came upon a Midnight Clear," as well as two original numbers written by the pair. "Listen, Listen" was one of the originals:

"Listen, Listen"

Christmas time is drawing near
Happy, joyful time of year
Snow is falling all around
Hear that special sound of snowflakes falling down…
Listen, listen
You will hear
Sounds of reindeer
In the air
Bringing love and bringing joy
And a very special toy
To every girl and boy.

Hodge said that someone approached her in 2010 and told her that the song she had written was one of her favorite Christmas numbers and that she wanted to cover the tune for an event at her church. "That was so special to me," she said. "It means a lot to know the kind of impact you have on people."

Not long afterward, Hodge was invited to appear in a parade in Columbus, Indiana, and invited Glaze to ride along with her. When they arrived at the parade and saw their car, someone had placed a sign on it that read "Janie and Cowboy Bob." Hodge recalls, "He wasn't Cowboy Bob...he was just Bob Glaze on the show, but for some reason, they put it on there."

Viewers enjoyed Bob's appearances on the *Janie* program, and when program director Don Tillman realized how popular Glaze had become, he called him into the office to announce that he would no longer appear on the show but asked, "How would you like your own show?"

A VERY LUCKY LADY

From 1972 to 1986, the *Janie* show was a staple in most households. Children checked in with their favorite hostess before catching the bus and could not wait to see her when she made her personal appearances around the state. The *Popeye and Janie* fan page on Facebook is full of memories from those who watched the show religiously, including a comment from Ellen Lippmann-Flemming, who remembered sending in her school picture and sitting very close to the TV so that she could see it when the camera panned Janie's picture board. "I couldn't believe it when I learned several years ago that Janie, Cowboy Bob and Sammy Terry were not known nationally," offered Claire Strayer. "People who did not know them missed out on a lot."

Once the show began being taped instead of broadcast live, Hodge was able to work five days a week in the classroom, make personal appearances on Saturdays and tape the show on Sunday, which worked out well for the children's groups who wanted to visit the set without missing school. She said that she was fortunate that her parents lived close by and could help keep an eye on her own children, as her husband was in real estate and worked on the weekends as well.

But in 1986, WTTV made the move to cut back on all live things, including the news and cartoon shows with live hosts, and Hodge became a

Another publicity photo from the "secret room" on the *Janie* show. *Courtesy of Brian (Jerry) Reynolds.*

casualty of a changing decade. Sadly, there is little footage of the *Janie* show that remains, as tapes were recycled whenever possible. Hodge said that that a few people have saved a few clips over the years, which she treasures, but she does not have a large catalogue of Janie memorabilia. "After the show was over, there was a mental change for me," she recalled. "I would still see things and think, 'Oh, we could use that.' I really missed the show for that first year. I still did a lot of personal appearances, and they still hire me and Bob to do personal appearances because it still brings people out...there is a huge feeling of nostalgia there."

One reunion event involving Hodge, Bob Carter (Sammy Terry) and Bob Glaze took place at the Indiana State Fairgrounds. When the show was announced, the stars had no idea what to expect in terms of an audience. In the end, the old Indiana University (IU) building was packed, and the hosts stayed for two hours, signing autographs and greeting the fans that never forgot them. Hodge recalled:

Today, Janie volunteers in the community with Indy Reads and the Indianapolis Symphony Orchestra. She also teaches bridge at Castleton Square Mall. *Author's private collection.*

They had to shut the doors because it was time for us to leave. We recently did a show at a little local theater, and so many people were there as well. We signed autographs and took pictures and talked with people, and they really do remember those little details of their lives that included us. We were part of their childhood. We were the ones who came out of the box and into their lives.

Matt, who is a professional musician in Indianapolis, said that he hopes to eventually bring the magic of the *Janie* show back to the airwaves through twenty-two-minute animated shorts that would appeal to kids as well as adults. "Several of the guys in my band are interested in helping to develop it, and we do have about five scripts on my laptop that we're playing with," he said. "We want to make it enjoyable and educational with the same level of class my mother brought to the screen…with the power of animation, Janie can go on to entertain a new generation of viewers. Mom loved the idea when I presented it to her."

Just don't expect Janie to revisit the small screen any time soon. While she loves making the occasional appearance, Hodge enjoys a semi-retired lifestyle that enables her to travel, volunteer with the Indy Reads organization, work with the Indianapolis Symphony Orchestra and play bridge with folks at Castleton Square Mall. She said that having enjoyed a career that enabled her to marry her passions of music and teaching was a blessing, and she never tires of the fans that still approach her and tell her how much they enjoyed the show. "Life has been good to me," she said. "I have moved on from being Janie, but I enjoyed it thoroughly, and I have truly been blessed."

CHAPTER 4

Behind the Scenes with the Puppet Master

We didn't realize we were doing anything special; when
you're in the middle of it, it's life.
—*Brian (Jerry) Reynolds*

At a very young age, Brian (Jerry) Reynolds knew his future was in television. As a middle-school student in Bloomington, he penned scripts that he hoped would turn into plotlines for *The Lucy Show* and longed for the day when he could take his passion and turn it into a full-time career.

He didn't have to wait long. After attending Roger's Elementary School and University High School, Reynolds entered Indiana University (IU) as a television production major, but unlike most college students, he had more than a little experience under his teenage belt. "I was hired by WTTV when I was seventeen years old," he said. "I was the youngest person ever to be hired at the station."

Reynolds parents were friends with a WTTV employee who worked in product development at the Bloomington studio, and when he heard about the youngster's interest in television, he invited Reynolds to the station for a visit. Reynolds said it proved to be a fortuitous meeting. When he arrived at the studio that Saturday morning, he said he thought he had died and gone to heaven, as he watched a taping of the *Hoosier Round Up* show (hosted by Bob Clark.) "It was a real TV studio," he said. It was real, but as he looked closely, Reynolds realized that WTTV was also a small operation. The can lights were made from real coffee cans that Dick Blair had cobbled together. The studio had only two or three real stage lights (on loan from the Indianapolis studio), and everything was shot in black-and-white. He didn't care though. It was still magical, and it was something he couldn't wait to be involved in. "I didn't even know that there was a Bloomington studio," Reynolds explained. "WTTV was on Channel 10 to begin with, and then they moved to Channel 4." He said that for a while, the station was run completely out of the Bloomington studio, but the powers-that-be ultimately realized that in order to grow, the station had to move to the Indianapolis market. "They had a split license for Bloomington and Indianapolis, so they had to keep the Bloomington studio open because that was the original city of license. And even though I watched Janie on the station, I had no idea there was a local studio."

Because the bulk of WTTV's programming was filmed in the Circle City, the Bloomington affiliate offered only a few shows, including a farm report, a daily half-hour talk show and fifteen to thirty minutes of news. Due to its close proximity to Indiana University, the school provided the station with footage that was broadcast through the Bloomington studio, as well as plenty of students who were able to get their feet wet in production without disrupting their class schedule. "It was all part-time," Reynolds recalled. "You'd get there at 4:30 in the morning, and you'd be done with the shows and off to breakfast by 7:30. It was perfect for a student."

After that first visit, Reynolds was hooked and determined to be a part of WTTV. He created art cards to show off his talent and literally begged station manager Dick Blair for a job. When Blair acquiesced, he had to drive the underage teenager to the school board building to get a work permit. He also agreed to drive the new studio assistant to work each day, as Reynolds didn't have a driver's license yet.

Reynolds began by doing art cards before moving on to lighting and camera work. Eventually, he began directing. He quickly learned that those who sat in the director's chair had to be experts at multitasking—they not only had to do the video but also had to shade the camera and run audio. It was the kind of thing that might be handled by three different people in Indianapolis, but Reynolds didn't mind the hard work. In fact, he thrived in it, saying that it was the best place to learn the craft. "I couldn't have asked for a nicer boss," he said. "Dick lived about five blocks away from me and would take me to work each morning. And when the shows were over, we would come back, pick up his kids and drive them to school. I don't know how many months we did that before I realized that I needed to get my license."

It was the kind of education that money can't buy, and Reynolds realized that his work at the studio far surpassed the classes he was taking at IU. He said he learned more in two weeks working at the station than he did in the five years he was enrolled at the university. Aside from the technical and business aspects of the business, he understood that those who were serious about a future in television had to be willing to do the grunt work that came along with creating a quality product. At WTTV, everyone was willing to start at the bottom and pitch in wherever necessary. No one started out as a vice-president or in other upper echelon–level roles. Even being in front of the camera was not a lucrative position. Bob Cook may have been the host of the *Hoosier Round Up* show, but he also did all of the commentary for the IU basketball games and worked at Johnson's Creamery as his day job. There was also a secretary at the station whose official job was to give the product development team what they needed, but in actuality, she primarily answered the phone. Reynolds said he was amazed at how many of the Channel 4 personalities had other positions outside of their work at the station in order to make ends meet, and he was also well aware of how unique his own situation was. "So much of what happened to me wouldn't happen today, but I was in the right place at the right time, and I wanted it so badly," Reynolds said. "After two summers of working with my father as an auto mechanic, I knew I wasn't going to follow in his footsteps…I was willing to do anything at the station. You have to be. Any student who thinks they are going to make that quantum leap from student to executive without something in between is fooling themselves."

A SHOW OF HIS OWN

Reynolds's talent did not go unnoticed around the studio. Station manager Don Tillman recognized the drive in his young employee, and he was eager to give him additional opportunities.

Tillman is credited by many who worked at WTTV as a mentor of sorts, as he believed in fostering the talent he uncovered in the studio and giving it a chance to shine. Like Reynolds, Tillman's broadcast career began in 1955 at WMRI-FM in Marion, Indiana, when he was still in high school. After graduation, he attended Indiana University for a brief period before transferring to Northwestern University, where he earned his degree in radio

Jerry Reynolds works on a script at the WTTV-4 Bloomington studios. At seventeen years old, he was the youngest person ever hired by the station. *Courtesy of Brian (Jerry) Reynolds.*

and television in 1961. During his college years, Tillman hosted a syndicated radio interview show called "Chicago on the Line" that could also be heard on stations such as WFMT in Chicago, WOWO in Fort Wayne and WTTW Channel 11 in Chicago. After a stint in the U.S. Army, Tillman returned to the Midwest, where he took positions at WTAF-TV in Marion and WQAD in Moline, Illinois.

Tillman eventually moved to WTTV, where he was the vice-president and station manager and was constantly on the lookout for new ideas and creative people who could make the station the best it could be. In 1972, Don Tillman felt that Reynolds had enough experience under his belt, and he tapped the nineteen-year-old to write and direct Janie Hodge's cartoon show, which was moving from its afternoon time slot to the mornings. It was a big responsibility, but Reynolds had already proven himself and was eager to do more writing. On top of that, he had already constructed a puppet pal for Hodge's afternoon program, so when Tillman made the offer, Reynolds said it was one he couldn't refuse: "Where in the world does a seventeen-year-old kid from Bloomington, Indiana, get to operate a camera or manage a floor and get handed his own show to write and produce? I am eternally grateful to Don Tillman for giving me opportunity after opportunity to do all of the things I wanted to do."

Moving *Janie's Treehouse* from the afternoons to the mornings meant eliminating the live studio audience associated with the show. While Hodge had been absent on maternity leave, Sally Jo Fridley had taken over the timeslot with *Sally Jo and Friends*. The show included a live audience, which meant that Hodge's new format could be taped. Tillman and Reynolds met with Hodge at the Key West Shrimp House on Madison Avenue to talk about the morning show, and while Hodge wasn't too keen on the idea of taping the program at first, she realized that taping the shows once a week would prevent her from having to race to the studio after school in order to make air time.

Reynolds went to work and wrote approximately seventy pages of material for the Janie pilot, which introduced cartoons, provided "storylines" for Janie and her puppet pals to banter with and included interview questions when a special guest was dropping by. He also ran several of the puppets on the stage and provided a number of voices for them as well.

Like Hodge, Reynolds wanted the show to have meaning beyond silliness, and the two worked hard to combine elements of education and fun into the *Janie* show. However, Reynolds said that there were times when he got carried away. "I would write these dramatic things that worried kids, carrying them out throughout several segments only to learn later that some of the kids who only watched between 7:30 and 8:30 before going to school had no idea what happened to Gilroy," he said. "I had to learn to reel it in a little bit and keep the bits shorter."

Taping the show meant that there were not as many gaffs as there might have been with a live show. But still, not everything went perfectly. When members of the Indianapolis Zoo stopped by with a rabbit for Janie to hold, the critter took off from Hodge's lap and hid behind the lighting board for half an hour. "Janie was afraid of animals, and I think they knew it…they gave her trouble every time," Reynolds said, noting that it wasn't long before Hodge's puppet Gilroy started doing all of the segments with the animals. "I got Janie to ride a horse once for about two seconds before she decided that Gilroy could ride the horse while she led it."

Of course, Gilroy had his issues as well. During a film wrap at a local park in which the gopher was to be shot looking as though he was swimming,

Left: The title page of the pilot *Janie* show script written by Jerry Reynolds. *Courtesy of Brian (Jerry) Reynolds*.

Below: Jerry Reynolds and the rest of the WTTV-4 crew set up the *Janie* show on location at the Indiana State Fairgrounds. *Courtesy of Brian (Jerry) Reynolds*.

Reynolds, who was underwater, slipped on the muddy bottom, and the puppet became waterlogged beyond repair. "We had to send poor Gilroy on a 'trip' to Florida for two weeks so that I could remake him quickly," Reynolds recalled.

Then there were the photos sent in by the viewers that bedecked Hodge's board and were panned as the show went to commercial breaks. Reynolds said that there were several crude drawings that looked different when viewed through a camera lens. A rudimentary rocket with two puffs of smoke at the bottom could easily be misinterpreted as something more anatomical when the camera panned. He recalls:

> *Janie was so trusting, but we knew that sometimes it wasn't kids sending them* [the drawings] *in. Of course, Cowboy Bob got the worst of it at times. He would get very suggestive letters from college students because, for a while, when he was on at noon, it was a big campus fad to watch Cowboy Bob. He was a local guy…he was handsome and wacky. The college kids responded to it as much as the younger viewers.*

Reynolds said that Channel 4 worked hard to create a symbiotic relationship with area organizations, and its children's programming offered mutual benefits for each group. He remembered shooting a week's worth of film at Conner Prairie with Janie dressed as a pioneer woman, as well as conducting live feeds at the Indiana State Fair and the Marion County Fair. "The live feeds at the fair were unique because invariably some kid would come along and rip off Gilroy's nose or something and force us to go to commercial," he laughed.

CREATIVE DYNAMOS

Reynolds's work was not limited to the *Janie* show. Like so many WTTV employees, he could be found on a number of sets, whether it was painting the backdrop on *Cowboy Bob's Corral*, creating the animated opening to *Debbie's Place* or illustrating the station newsletter. At one point, Don Tillman was so impressed with Reynolds that he pitched the idea of having him host his own show, playing the part of a forest ranger in a fire tower drawing pictures. "I have no idea why they were contemplating another

Debbie Bays was the host of *Debbie's Place*, a short-lived afternoon cartoon show. *Courtesy of Brian (Jerry) Reynolds.*

hosted show, but it was horrible," he said, laughing at the memory. "While I do have the sense that I have some talent and can do voices and behind-the-scenes stuff, I do not have the ability to do what Janie did—to look into the camera and be real. I was so nervous. The pilot never aired, and I don't

Jerry Reynolds, Janie Hodge and the rest of the crew film a *Janie* show segment on a train at Indiana Beach. *Courtesy of Brian (Jerry) Reynolds.*

think it was ever mentioned again. Thankfully, no footage exists so there is no evidence of it."

Matt Hodge remembers Reynolds as one of the many creative dynamos responsible for much of the success of the *Janie* show. "Jerry was really the do-it-all guy on the stage, but nobody ever saw his face," Hodge recalled. "Some of my fondest memories at WTTV are of the two puppeteers that worked on my mother's show. Jerry not only made all of the puppets by hand, operated and voiced them, but he also did all of the illustrations of the Janie character that appeared on the show and wrote the script, formatting my mother's and his own ideas into a cohesive unit."

In addition to Tillman, Hodge and Dick Blair, Reynolds said there were many people who made his time at WTTV so enjoyable. Among them was floor manager Peggy McCelland, who made what could have been a fairly unpleasant experience so much better. McCelland was an Indiana native who began her broadcasting career in 1976 after graduating from Ball State University. Originally hired as a member of the production department, she worked her way up the ladder to become the production manager of the station in 1987. Reynolds said that when McCelland came to the station, there were only two women on the studio crew at the time. Channel 4 understood that the children's personalities and Sammy Terry were the celebrities of the station, even if the crew didn't always take the programs seriously. Reynolds recalled:

> *Peggy McCelland came in and treated those shows with dignity and respect. She knew these shows had value, and she used her own kids as a mirror. I liked her a lot, and she quickly became the floor manager of choice to work with. She really bridged that gap, and she had done a tremendous job to preserve as much of the history of that station as possible. She even found the Gilroy and Silly Snake puppets. When I went out to see Janie's appearance in Greenfield a couple of years ago, Peggy spotted me in the audience and asked me to come back and work the puppets just like old times. Janie and I fell into our old routine as though no time had passed.*

A SPECIAL TIME

Looking back on his time at the station, Reynolds said that he is very proud to have been part of such a special time in local television and that he's proud of the work he did there. In 1976, he flew out to the Hanna-Barbera Studios in California to interview William Hanna himself. When Reynolds showed him the animated opening he created for the short-lived *Debbie's Place* cartoon show consisting of all of the classic Hanna-Barbera characters marching on parade, Hanna asked if he had permission to use the trademarked likenesses. Without skipping a beat, Reynolds said that he was under the impression that because the station had purchased the cartoon package, they were entitled to use the characters for promotional purposes. "He said, 'We'll let it go this time,'" Reynolds laughed. "I'm still pretty proud of that opening. I went to incredible effort to animate that opening sequence, and no sooner did I finish it when the hostess' husband got a job out west and she quit to be with him."

Reynolds was offered a job as an assistant animator at the famed studio, but it was then that he realized what he really wanted was to start a production company of his own. In 1979, Reynolds left WTTV to start

The *Channel 4 Informer* was the staff newsletter illustrated by Jerry Reynolds that told all of the news around the station. *Courtesy of Peggy Powis.*

Perennial Pictures with fellow Channel 4 alum Russ Harris. He didn't sever all ties, however. The two filmed a sitcom pilot at the Bloomington studio, animated Mercer Meyer's *Just Me and My Dad*, developed *Alien's Next Door* for the Disney Channel and created O. Ratz for the Hanna-Barbera *What a Cartoon!* series.

O. Ratz is the story of an unfortunate rodent and his sidekick, Dave D. Fly, who endure a number of mishaps in an effort to find warmth on a cold winter night. The animated short was created at Perennial's Indianapolis studio and recorded in Hollywood and features the voices of Harvey Korman (*Carol Burnett Show*), Marvin Kaplan (*Alice*) and Nancy Dussault (*Too Close for Comfort*). "We were reading people for the title character, and we weren't finding what we wanted. We even had a note saying that we wanted a Harvey Korman type, and eventually they said, 'Why don't you just get Harvey Korman?' I didn't know we could do that!"

Reynolds's work has also allowed him to work with the likes of Rob Paulson (Pinky of *Pinky and the Brain*) and June Foray of the *Rocky & Bullwinkle Show*. "She was ninety-two when she came in to work with us, and when she arrived at the studio, she immediately said 'Holy smokes, Bullwinkle!' in her Rocky voice. I was gone. Talk about a legend!" (Among her credits, Foray was also the voice of Jokey Smurf, Natasha on *The Bullwinkle Show*, Grandmother Fa in Disney's *Mulan* and Karen in *Frosty the Snowman*.)

Matt Hodge said that when Reynolds left the station, Jim Dicks took over as the lead puppeteer. "He did remarkably well duplicating the voices and personalities that Jerry established…people would be hard pressed to notice the transition, Hodge noted. "Jim was also a musician, and I remember that he and his band, Iron Horse, played one of my mother's parties, giving guests flawless renditions of favorites like the Oak Ridge Boys and Alabama."

Like his early mentor and fellow IU alum Madelyn Pugh Davis (*I Love Lucy*, *The Lucy Show*, *Here's Lucy*), Reynolds said that he didn't realize at the time that he was part of a unique era in Indiana television history that has generated a popular resurgence in recent years. "We didn't realize we were doing anything special," he said. "When you are in the middle of it, it's life. Madelyn didn't know that her greatest success would come so early or that *I Love Lucy* would do what it did. You take it for granted, and then when it's over, and the years have passed, you realize how special it was. I have a lot of gratitude for my years at Channel 4, but I still think the best is yet to come!

CHAPTER 5

Rib Ticklin' Fun

Keep smiling, don't forget to take your naps and if you can't say anything nice, don't say anything at all.
—"Cowboy Bob" Glaze

Years before Woody the Cowboy warbled "You've got a Friend in Me" in the movie *Toy Story*, television viewers depended on other cowboy heroes to act as a model of good behavior, impart sage advice and ride off into the sunset (guitar in hand, of course.) Children cheered for Roy Rogers, Gene Autry and other singing cowboys, but Indiana children had one of their own: "Cowboy Bob" Glaze.

Born in the Oklahoma panhandle in 1942, Glaze moved to Indiana with his mother and sister when he was only twelve years old. He attended Culver Military Academy, graduating in 1960, and was accepted to Indiana University, where he briefly majored in French and Italian. "What was I thinking there?" he laughed.

A natural musician and a self-described show business "ham," Glaze recorded a single that found its way to Chicago, and before long, the student left college behind in order to chase down his musical dreams in the Windy City. He took a job on WBBM's Mal Bellair's *Music Wagon*, and when he was not on the air, Glaze served as the opening act for a number of well-known artists, including Harry Belafonte, the Chad Mitchell Trio and Connie Stevens. Glaze recalled that *Silver Screen* magazine made a big deal of his connection to the actress/singer known for the novelty hit song "Kookie,

Kookie, Lend Me Your Comb" and her appearances on the television series *77 Sunset Strip*, but the two were never linked romantically. "All I can say to that is I wish!" he laughed. "She was a delightful lady, and I was very starstruck with her.

After a year and a half of living in Chicago, Glaze found his passion in broadcast media and returned to IU in order to complete his education. He earned a degree in radio and television and accepted a position as a cameraman at the WTTV studio in Bloomington, where he worked on Bob Cook's *RFD-4* and *The Bernie Nicolei Breakfast Show*. He later relocated to the Indianapolis studios, where he was thrilled to work on *Nightmare Theater*, *The Billie Boucher Show*, *The Jim Gerard Show* and the Indiana Department of Natural Resources (DNR) nature program *Indiana Outdoors*. Like everyone else who worked around the station, Glaze learned to do a little bit of everything. He served as a crewmember, director, producer and an on-screen personality as well, portraying Harley Slarp, the boyfriend of Mary Ellen Reed, who hosted *Popeye's Diner*. He also made cameo appearances on a number of other programs. If being behind the camera was exciting, being in front of the camera was even more so. "I loved every minute of it," he recalled. "I wormed my way onto anyone's show."

COWBOY BOB

In Janie Hodge, Glaze found a kindred spirit in the music teacher who loved to ask members of her crew to sing a song or two on her show. Glaze was only too happy to comply when she extended the invitation, and before long, he was a fixture on *Janie's Treehouse*. Not only did the two film a commercial for Mountain Dew, but they also recorded a Christmas album and made a number of personal appearances together, including the infamous Columbus Parade, in which Glaze was unwittingly christened "Cowboy Bob."

Glaze said that he was riding high on his newfound fame, so it came as a blow when station manager Don Tillman pulled the plug on his *Janie* appearances. But he didn't have to be sad for long, because Tillman told him that he wanted Glaze to replace Reed as the host of the *Lunch Time Theater* show. Glaze was overjoyed. "Talk about going from tears to joy!" he exclaimed.

Glaze recognized that it was Hodge's generosity that allowed him to display his on-air talent in such a way that gave him an opportunity to host

Janie Hodge and Bob Glaze in the early 1960s as the pair recorded their Christmas album. Bob was a regular guest on Hodge's show before he was given his own show. *Courtesy of Matt and Janie Hodge.*

his own show. "I owe Janie a supreme debt, because if it hadn't been for her, Cowboy Bob might never have happened," he noted. "She allowed me to be on her show and essentially gave me that opportunity."

The next step was to create an image that the viewing audience could bond with. Several options were considered, including a clown, but Glaze thought back to those cattle ranchers he saw as he grew up in Oklahoma and chose to stay true to his roots. He also remembered the nickname he'd "earned" at the parade in Columbus and decided that a cowboy would be the best character for his show. "What else could I be except Cowboy Bob?" he mused. "Besides, it kind of sounded like it went together."

Others thought so as well. Little did the station know that when they gave the green light to Glaze's new moniker, there was another "Cowboy Bob" in the entertainment world. "Cowboy Bob" Ellis was a famous wrestler from San Angelo, Texas, known for his sleeper hold and underhook suplex moves before finishing off his opponent with a bulldog headlock. For years, Glaze received a number of misdirected letters intended for the fighter, including some sent by very forthright women. "You should have seen some of the letters I received," he laughed, noting that there was also a restaurant in Brownsburg named

A caricature drawing of Cowboy Bob and his dog Rusty O'Toole by Hagerstown resident Joe Klemann. *Courtesy of Bob Glaze.*

Cowboy Bob's that everyone thought was affiliated with him. "I learned about that when I got a call from the IRS reading me the riot act. It took me an hour to convince them that I wasn't that Cowboy Bob."

Glaze hit the airwaves on January 7, 1970, as the host of the newly renamed *Chuckwagon Theater*. Author Tim Hollis noted that it might have been a little late in the game for a station to launch a "cowboy" show, but Glaze's show proved to be hipper than the "Uncle Bob" Hardy of the past. The show was a big hit with the young viewing audience, and Glaze took a hands-on approach with all aspects of the production. He chose all of the cartoons himself and said he often micromanaged his crew, but he was quick to point out that they were largely responsible for the success of the show. Youngsters were drawn to the content, as well as Glaze's cowboy persona and easy-going nature. Packed with cartoons, corny jokes and plenty of fun, Glaze's show was designed to entertain children during the lunch hour and served as a surrogate babysitter for a few minutes out of the day. The show provided him countless opportunities to explore different areas of his creativity. A major sponsor of the program was Choc-Ola, a bottled soft drink that boasted a rich chocolate flavor with a hint of cola. Having worked with the brothers who wrote the famous "We Bring Good Things to Light" jingle for General Electric (GE), Glaze tried his hand at jingle writing, penning a successful campaign for Choc-Ola. "Somehow I managed to land a contract where I got residuals instead of a lump sum, realizing that I would take a lot less over time and hoping it would pay off in the end. It did for a couple of years. I was getting a major check every month. Choc-Ola went out of business, but I heard that it's being served over at Rock-Cola Café on Brookville Road in Indianapolis," he said.

Chuckwagon Theater hadn't been on the air too long when Glaze began to realize the tremendous influence he held over his young audience. At one point, a young mother wrote in to ask Glaze to please remind her son to take his nap after the show was over. He complied and was deluged with mail from other Hoosier mothers begging him to continue. It became a part of his daily sign off: "Keep smiling, don't forget to take your naps and if you can't say anything nice, don't say anything at all." Joe Klemann of Hagerstown noted, "Cowboy Bob was the kind of cowboy I wanted to be. He…could actually ride a horse and swing a lasso, gave us three great cartoons and made us part of his Chuckwagon Theater each day at noon. Today's movie and television cowboys could learn a lot from Cowboy Bob!"

In addition to the show's charismatic host and the cartoon fare, kids couldn't get enough of Cowboy Bob's cast of sidekicks, including Tumbleweed the dog, horses Skye and Windjammer, Cooky, Pony Express rider Harley Slarp and, of course, Sourdough the Singing Biscuit, which came about after an audio glitch during the live show. As Glaze bantered with Cooky (his off-screen alter ego), he dropped a prop biscuit, expecting to hear the cued shattering of glass in reference to Cooky's lack of culinary skills. Instead, the sound that piped through the studio was a track of Glaze singing. I couldn't stop because it was live, so all I could say was, 'Oh look, Cooky, you made a singing biscuit!'" he laughed. "I went on and cued the cartoon, and the next thing you know, I am getting mail from kids who want to hear the singing biscuit again. I drew a face onto a dried up KFC biscuit and used it for five years before [using] the hand puppet people remember from the 1980s. We made a big thing about unveiling the new and improved Sourdough. With a live show though, you just had to wing it sometimes."

Cowboy Bob Club members subscribe to the

Cowboy Bob Creed,

as printed below:

(1) I will be helpful and courteous to all persons.

(2) I will respect my parents, teachers, brothers, and sisters.

(3) I will follow a code of good conduct.

(4) I will at all times be a good citizen.

(5) I will be respectful of others and their privileges.

A vintage Burger Chef Cowboy Bob Club membership card. Glaze said that Burger Chef was a major sponsor of his show, and he loved clowning on camera with his Fun Meal. *Author's private collection.*

Another famous episode concerned the Joke Barrel. Similar to Janie's Mailboxer, who presented her with letters and jokes from viewers, the Joke Barrel contained a myriad of riddles and jokes and laughed whenever Glaze lifted the lid to read one on the air. They weren't always vetted for appropriateness, as Glaze found out when one day he read "Why does the ocean roar?" to Sourdough, who in turn responded, "I don't know, why?" Without missing a beat, Glaze read the punch line: "You'd roar too if you had crabs on your bottom!" It was just another example of how live television often led to gaffs. "I loved the '70s because everything was live, and that was a joy. If you screwed up—and we did—you laughed it off and kept going."

Matt Hodge said Glaze, as the singing cowboy, was never afraid to tell a terribly corny joke or poke fun at himself, but aside from his on-screen persona, he was a very focused show director and accomplished musician who took the lightheartedness of his act very seriously. He recalled:

> *I had the great pleasure of participating in many of the live shows, and before each show, we would sit down and hammer out a game plan. Bob and I would*

Bob Carter as Sammy Terry, Gail Butterfield, Bob Glaze and an unknown woman mug for a snapshot at the WTTV-4 studio on Bluff Road. *Courtesy of SammyTerryNightmares.com.*

tune up our guitars, and Janie would help us work out the vocal arrangements and tell us where the jokes were to be inserted. I have always been impressed with how good Bob's musical ear is. He still only uses one tuning fork and tunes the rest of his guitar strings to that one note. It's quite amazing how fast and accurate he is!

FINDING HIS COWGIRL

In 1972, Glaze's work at WTTV brought him another happy surprise: his future wife. Gail Butterfield attended Manuel High School and lived on Indianapolis' Southside when she first met Glaze in 1970 at the age of sixteen. She attended the Crossroads Rehabilitation Easter Egg hunt at the Governor's Residence with her father, who suggested that she introduce herself to celebrity attendee Cowboy Bob. She did, he was gracious and the incident was forgotten. Two years later, she was hired by the station as a film

Bob Glaze proposes to his girlfriend, Gail Butterfield, off the coast of Cozumel. *Courtesy of Bob Glaze.*

editor and spent her lunch breaks watching Glaze on the air. Before long, he started bringing her out on set. "We called Gail 'Wrangler Gail,'" said Brian Reynolds, who was on the production crew for Glaze's show.

It didn't take long for romance to spark. Though Gail was only employed at WTTV for six months, Glaze deemed it a fateful experience that brought them together. "I swore I would not get married until I was convinced that this was the right person. My mother had divorced young...so [Gail and I] dated for three and half years," he recalled, noting a few dates in which he was convinced the young woman would dump him. "Finally, my sister said, 'If you don't marry her, you're going to lose her.' I realized she was right."

Glaze arranged to travel with Butterfield to Cozumel on a scuba-diving trip during which he planned to propose. On the last day of the adventure, the duo dove sixty feet below the surface, and Glaze popped "the question" on an underwater white board. "Fortunately, she said yes," he said. They have been married ever since and enjoy a variety of activities, including scuba diving, wind surfing, cycling, horseback riding and rowing.

Stop, Drop and Roll

Glaze's chuck wagon moved to the mornings in 1980 as the lead in to the *Janie* show. Renamed *Cowboy Bob's Corral*, Glaze filmed the opening riding sequence behind the WTTV studios and penned the theme song, which can still be recited by many of his former viewers:

The hitchin' post is waitin' 'round the bend.
My weary ride is comin' to an end.
Gonna stop and wrap myself around
The best rib-ticklin' in this town,
Where laughin' is in style.
I think I'm going to stop awhile and smile.
It's time for Cowboy Bob's Corral.
Out where a pal is a pal.
We've got good times for you,
And lots of things to do.
So come along, my cowboy buckaroo-oo-oo-oo-oo!

The show still featured popular Hanna-Barbera favorites such as Yogi Bear, Snagglepuss and Huckleberry Hound, along with music and special guests like Handy the Helping Hand. It also became a platform for issues that were close to Glaze's heart, such as animal rights and other community concerns, aired in public service announcements (PSAs) that became imbedded in the public consciousness.

One particular campaign that became synonymous with the show was a PSA for the Indianapolis Fire Department in which Glaze and his trusty dog Tumbleweed reminded everyone to "Stop, Drop and Roll" if their clothes ever caught on fire. Crawling on her belly and feeling the door with her paw, Tumbleweed also illustrated what to do if a viewer ever found himself in a room full of smoke. "She was so smart," Glaze recalled of the dog who was once the runt of a neighbor's litter, went on to become a TV star and died at the ripe age of sixteen. "Poor Tumbleweed," Reynolds said, remembering the

The Hoffmeier Weiner Company was a sponsor of the *Cowboy Bob's Corral* and offered these promotional pins during public appearances. *Courtesy of Bob Glaze.*

station's furry friend. "She had this one air-conditioned area where she stayed all day because Bob had so much to do around the station. Sometimes I think he was in that cowboy outfit all day. However, when the weather was nice, Tumbleweed would get to go out back by the chuck wagon."

Glaze and Tumbleweed were so associated with the "Stop, Drop and Roll" procedure that many viewers assumed it was Glaze's invention rather than fire-safety protocol. To this day, the "Stop, Drop and Roll" campaign is one of the most frequently asked questions on Glaze's website, and he is proud to have partnered with the fire department to raise an awareness of fire safety and to have made such a difference in the lives of so many people. "It saved a lot of lives," Glaze remembered.

Glaze said there was a woman who recalled the PSA at a critical time when she was in an accident and thrown from her motorcycle. Just before the fuel tank exploded, she was able to roll away, sustaining only minor injuries. When Glaze heard about the incident, he made a personal visit to her hospital bedside.

It wasn't his last trip to the hospital to see a fan. One of the first sponsors for his show was the Marhoefer Packing Company, which provided Glaze with Happy Weiner inflatable hotdogs to give away as an on-air promotion. Each week, Cowboy Bob selected a winning viewer to receive the prize. The mother of a five-year-old terminally ill child in Bloomington wrote to the show to tell Glaze that her daughter's dying wish was to have a Marhoefer Happy Weiner inflatable. He brought the balloon to her personally. "I hand delivered it to her a week before she passed," he said, his voice breaking with emotion. "The look on her face…she was so happy, but I was frustrated because there was nothing more I could do for her. We just wanted to make everything so personal for our viewers, whether it was mentioning their names on the air, showing the pictures they sent in or visiting with them at appearances. There was no way they wouldn't watch the show."

Glaze's fans may not know this, but they were directly responsible for saving their favorite cowboy's life. During one show, the camera cut to the set too soon and, Glaze was caught smoking onscreen. It didn't take long for fans to write in and beg Glaze to quit. He recalled, "They sent me the nicest letters saying, 'We really wish you wouldn't do that. We love you, and we want you around for a long time.' I quit right then and there, cold turkey. I did it for them."

LIKE BEING ON CARSON

The fans meant everything to Cowboy Bob, and he meant everything to them. If watching *Cowboy Bob's Corral* or seeing their hero in person was a big deal, being on the show was like hitting the big time. No matter if you were part of a scout troop, a crowd shot at the state fairgrounds or filling a hay wagon at the pumpkin patch with Happy the Helping Hand, Cowboy Bob viewers were thrilled to appear on camera while their friends and family watched back home.

Adam Roth was just five years old when he appeared on *Cowboy Bob's Corral*, having won a prize for his "Be Kind to Animals Week" drawing. The caption on his picture was, "Let your moose smell the flowers." Though he has no memory of being on the show, Adam's wife, Kate, said it was cute to watch her husband's appearance on the show and that the story has become legendary in their family:

It was adorable to see him wiggling in the background amidst the crowd of kids. Finally, all of the kids were showing off their artwork that had won the prize for their age group, but his tiny voice came out loud and clear as he walked by holding up his picture. He was just a blip on the show, but everyone in the family has really sweet memories of the experience.

Roth's mother, Jill, said that her son was nervous and excited to be on the show and that as a parent, she appreciated how the local host would talk about events going on around the city, announce birthdays on air and help viewers feel like they were part of the show. "It was always fun to hear your kids' names announced," she said. "As for the poster and the art contest, I don't know where he got the idea of the moose. Have you ever seen a moose in Indiana? Maybe it was his dry wit, but I believe he was being sincere. Anyway, he is almost finished with his fine arts degree from the Arts Institute of Indianapolis, and I like to think that Cowboy Bob had a small part in that."

For Rusty Ammerman, appearing on Cowboy Bob's show was like being on *The Tonight Show* with Johnny Carson. As a child growing up in Connersville, Indiana, his favorite stations were WTTV-4 in Indianapolis and WXIX in Cincinnati because they had all of the cool creature features, syndicated reruns and cartoon shows that he loved. He also loved watching *Championship Wrestling* with his father and seeing Dick the Bruiser, Pepper Gomez and Wilbur Snider fight each other in the ring. "They were true legends of the sport and really only one generation removed from Gorgeous George and those guys," he said. "I remember my father taking me to one of the wrestling matches where it was announced that "Cowboy Bob" Ellis would appear. I was so disappointed to learn that it wasn't the Cowboy Bob I knew from TV."

Ammerman loved *Cowboy Bob's Corral* and quickly learned to mimic many of the voices he heard on the Hanna-Barbera cartoons, including those of Snagglepuss, Oggie Doggie, Quickdraw McGraw and Milton the Monster. Like many of Cowboy Bob's other viewers, he couldn't distinguish the local program from something on a national level. Television was the great equalizer. Surely Cowboy Bob knew everyone else in the business, and Ammerman knew that an appearance on his show could lead to that big break.

When he was sixteen, Ammerman called the station in hopes of appearing on the Cowboy Bob show. He'd been performing magic for six months under the name Dr. Illusion and was ready to show off his skills for a larger audience. To his surprise, Glaze took the call, and when he heard the teenager's pitch, he asked if he had any Halloween-themed tricks that he could perform on air. "I did what any good performer would do," Ammerman laughed. "I said yes and then set about figuring out which tricks would translate."

Glaze invited him to the studio to film his segments, and Ammerman cut classes in order to drive to Indianapolis only to find a deserted parking lot when he arrived. Worried that he had made a mistake, he was thinking about leaving when Glaze pulled up in his pick-up truck, greeted him warmly and let him into the studio. "It was a rectangular room with the different sets scattered around so that the camera could turn 360 degrees. I saw the news set, Cowboy Bob's set, the talk-show set…everything except Sammy Terry's set, which was behind a curtain," he said.

Ammerman filmed several three-minute segments that included a floating ball, a witches' house illusion and a disappearing skull. He had such a good time and performed so well that he was convinced it would lead to that big call from David Copperfield. While that didn't happen, Ammerman, who now lives in Fort Wayne, does make his living as a professional magician. He has performed at the legendary Magic Castle and in forty-three states and nine countries. However, he said that his appearance on *Cowboy Bob's Corral* resonates with him as a pivotal moment in his career. "The thought that he would say 'No' didn't occur to me," Ammerman noted. "He was very generous to let me come on the show and perform. I thought he was the biggest star at the time, and that affable personality of his really demonstrated what it means to be a professional in the entertainment industry. It's a lesson I take on the road with me to this day."

A Moment in Time

Although *Cowboy Bob's Corral* ended in the late 1980s as more cable channels began focusing on twenty-four-hour children's programming, Glaze has been anything but idle. He can be found puttering around his Morgantown home, working out at the Barbara B. Jordan YMCA in Martinsville or on the water at Eagle Creek Park with the Culver Alumni Rowing Crew. "Rowing is a team sport that teaches you how to synchronize your movements with those of your teammates," he said. "It's the kind of sport that allows you to develop both physically and emotionally."

In 1996, fellow Culver alum Bob Evans (not that Bob Evans) asked if Glaze would be interested in forming a rowing crew of Culver alums. Glaze jumped at the chance to get involved. "It was like a dream come true," Glaze said. "I had been away from it for so long, and I really wanted to do it again." Together, the pair, along with Glaze's wife, Gail, and Culver classmate Don Nixon, reached out to all of the alums in the area they could think of and approached the Indianapolis Rowing Center at Eagle Creek to arrange practice space at their facility, which was built in 1987 for the Pan Am Games.

Though the group is small and some members are more active than others, Glaze said the Culver Club of Indianapolis Rowing Team has stayed alive for more than fifteen years and is always seeking new members. "We are always looking for those who have a Culver connection, but we've also supplemented our numbers by recruiting almost anyone who is healthy, willing to row and can spell Culver," he said. "We are a pretty laid back group that is not competitive. We just like to get out and row for the fun of it, and we are capable of teaching anyone who might want to give rowing a try." But he's never too busy to revisit the magical era that brought *Chuckwagon Theater* and *Cowboy Bob's Corral* to viewers everywhere. He said that the 1970s were a time when a cartoon host could mug with a Burger Chef Fun Meal or sip on Choc-Ola live on the air—a time before hosts were forbidden from doing so and when such actions caused stations to question the validity of their on-screen character personalities.

According to Billy Ingram, author of *TV Party: Television's Untold Stories*, a group of concerned parents formed Action for Children's Television (ACT) in order to try and clean up the sad state of kids' television. Determined to rid the airwaves of all negative influences, ACT pressured the National Association of Broadcasters (NAB) to create sweeping reforms. In 1972, the NAB amended its code as follows:

> *Children's program hosts or primary cartoon characters shall not be used to deliver commercial messages within or adjacent to the programs which feature such hosts or cartoon characters. This provision shall also apply to lead-ins to commercials when such lead-ins contain sell copy or employ endorsement of the product by program host or primary cartoon character.*

The text of the amendment all but erased incentive for local sponsors to buy time during the kiddie hour, and it wasn't long before stations realized that without the sponsors, there was little reason to pay someone to host the program. "It was much more lucrative for a station when the host could help sell the product," Reynolds said. "After everything was restricted, stations wondered if they even needed the hosts anymore." "I saw nothing wrong with having some fun and hawking the sponsor's product a bit," Glaze added.

Glaze also loved the meet-and-greets at county and state fairs, during which he broadcast live remotes and had the chance to banter with his fans.

Left: "Cowboy Bob" Glaze has never stopped performing. Here he tells jokes and shares stories at the Irving Theater in 2010. *Author's private collection.*

Below: Rusty O'Toole, Vincent Johnson-Horan and Cowboy Bob Glaze pose for a photo in Glaze's Morgantown home. *Author's private collection.*

Like Janie, he had a lengthy waiting list of kids who wanted to visit on the air, and he loved being able to shake hands with them, smile and tell the fans how much he appreciated their loyalty. "My brother and I were lucky to get some airtime at the state fair shows in the early '80s…it was very cool," said Anderson native Benjamin Schott.

Kelly (Krout) Kirby said that Cowboy Bob was a regular part of her morning routine while getting ready for school. "I couldn't wait to watch Cowboy Bob and Janie over a bowl of Sugar Pops. They don't make shows like that nowadays," she posted on Facebook.

The downside, of course, is that nothing was saved. Fans who have requested a compilation DVD of the WTTV-4 shows may have a long wait, as few clips have been preserved. Glaze said that none of the shows were archived due to the expense and space that storage would have required at the time. "You have to understand that in the '70s, the videotape that we used was on these huge, wide reels" he said. "They couldn't save all of that stuff, and they didn't even bother. It was always quick and dirty. It never occurred to anyone that someone would want to see it someday. Now, of course, you can store mountains of stuff in an envelope, but back then, you couldn't, and it's a shame."

A few classic clips have been salvaged, thanks in part to the diligence of Peggy McCelland, who not only produced and directed various WTTV shows but also became the erstwhile historian of the station. "She was a workaholic who did anything and everything around there," Glaze said. "She was the best producer and historian there ever was."

Thanks to a renewed interest in the classic WTTV-4 character personalities, Glaze is working on a number of endorsements and personal appearances that will enable him to revisit his beloved role for years to come. He said:

> *The character I tried to portray was that of a surrogate—a brother or a father for some of these kids—because some of them probably didn't have a lot of guidance. I just knew what I felt in my heart would be good for the kids. A little bit of knowledge and a whole lot of fun—we combined it together, and it seemed to pay off. Today they talk about thinking outside of the box. We got out of the box. The kids would know us on TV, and then they would also see us all around the state doing personal appearances. So many times they'd ask, "How did you get out of the TV?" You know, how sweet is that?*

CHAPTER 6

Smooth Sailing

Until tomorrow, Smoo-oo-th Sailing!
—*Peggy Nicholson,* Peggy & Popeye

For Peggy (Nicholson) Powis, earning her place in WTTV history was as simple as winning her audition, an audition her friend dared her to show up for. "Had I set out to do it, it never would have happened," she said.

Born in 1950, the former Terre Haute resident was no stranger to Channel 4. Her father was a sales person for the station, and she was a big fan of WTTV personalities such as Les the Cartoonist and Chesty the Clown, who introduced Little Rascal shorts on their shows. After graduating from Gerstmeyer Technical High School, she enrolled in Indiana State University (ISU), where she majored in speech/communication and theater, appearing in a number of productions through ISU and the Terre Haute Community Theater. She also spent a season with the Happiness Bag Players, a traveling children's theater company that specialized in interactive performances. "The audience—they were both children and adults—was involved with the programs. They would suggest topics to the actors and even become part of the play," Nicholson said in a WTTV press release.

In 1972, with her well-honed adaptability and improvisational skills, Nicholson relocated to Indianapolis, where she took a position in the advertising department of L.S. Ayres & Co. She also served as a community outreach worker for the City of Indianapolis and as a volunteer with the Indianapolis Public Schools. She was also a member of the Talent Resource

Bank, where she visited a variety of schools conducting workshops on the subject of "Poetry, Rhythm and Rhyme." Just prior to joining WTTV, Nicholson spent a year with the Human Relations Consortium, a federally funded project working with parents in the area of school desegregation, and launched a Reader's Theater program that performed at meetings and private parties throughout Indianapolis and Terre Haute.

However, Peggy's friend believed that her bubbly personality, youth and enthusiasm would be a great fit for children's television and arranged the audition that Nicholson begrudgingly agreed to attend. Although she lacked the on-air experience of some of the other hopefuls, including a veteran TV personality from Cincinnati, WTTV program director Don Tillman couldn't help but notice the special brand of magic Nicholson brought to the screen, and he hired her to take over the 3:30–4:30 p.m. afternoon cartoon timeslot previously home to *Debbie's Place*. "Debbie had taken over from Sally Jo, who had taken the timeslot when Janie moved to mornings. When I became the afternoon delight, the show premiered as *Peggy's World*," she said.

Peggy's World debuted on July 7, 1975, continuing the WTTV tradition of children's programming. Nicholson was responsible for keeping the show within the time constraints with the live wraps and other features, while Jerry (Brian) Reynolds designed the set and provided illustrations for the show. "Peggy and I are a lot alike in a lot of ways, and I just love her," said Reynolds. "I met her as she was coming in and being introduced around the station as the new kids' host, and together we designed the new set. We always say that she is the 1950 model and that I am the 1952 model. She was always so much fun!"

Unlike Cowboy Bob and Janie's morning cartoon shows, Nicholson's afternoon cavalcade included a live peanut gallery–style audience. Each day, the children would march in, appear on camera and say their names before "grabbing a button" (the Nicholson term for "take your seat") and settling in for an afternoon of fun and folly. During the show, while the audience at home watched the latest adventures of their cartoon favorites, those in the studio had the chance to run cameras, work with the crew and learn a little behind-the-scenes TV magic. "We allowed kids to come behind the scenes…wind the zoom, tilt and pan [all] with the help of a crew member," she noted. "A few of the directors also helped kids see what could be done with a chroma key. Who knows how many digital engineers were first tantalized by a Channel 4 visit! It could not have happened any place else."

Though he wasn't part of the *Peggy's World* audience, the crewmembers at the station made a big impression on Matt Hodge as well. When he was lolling around the studio, he recalled that the guys in the control booth wearing headsets looked as though they were at the helm of the Starship Enterprise, and the floor crew kept an easy-going mood on the set. "They were always very generous with their knowledge of how the behemoth machines captured the images and sent them to our television homes." Hodge made friends with a man by the name of Bud Bray. Bray and his wife were expecting a baby, providing an opportunity for the guys in the crew to come up with joke baby names that would play on Bud's surname. "I quickly chimed in with my own suggestion of "Om Bray" (after the Spanish word *hombre* for man). The laughter that followed made me feel like one of the gang," he said.

Nicholson realized that she could accommodate more guests on her show if she taped segments that could be used at a later date. Not only could she cut the ever-growing waiting list down considerably, but she was also able to do three shows in the time it took to do one live performance, which freed up studio time for more profitable programs. In addition, taping the show meant that her guests could watch themselves at a later date. Nicholson said she realized early on that she came in at the end of an era as far

as children's programming was concerned, but she was determined to make the most of it while she was there. By the end of her run, there was no audience of any kind—just her and the crew. "The final shows at the state fair closed the era," she said.

A publicity shot of Peggy Nicholson just after she was hired to replace Debbie Bays at WTTV. *Courtesy of Peggy Powis.*

Nicholson's time on the air with WTTV was not without its controversial moments. When *Peggy's World* segued into the *Popeye & Peggy* show, the spinach-eating sailor came under fire by mothers who were chagrined at the amount of violence displayed in the cartoon shorts. "The station had bowed to discontent and removed Popeye from the lineup," Nicholson said. "But it wasn't long before Popeye was back…he was a favorite with the kids watching, and as we all knew, we lived and died by the numbers of kids watching. When Popeye came back, the name of the show was changed to herald his return, and the numbers went up." The show's name change prompted her to don a sailor hat on air and start closing the show with her signature signoff: "So, until tomorrow, Smoo-oo-th Sailing!"

If Nicholson's afternoon show was a huge hit with the fans, the personal touch she infused into her appearances and correspondence made an even bigger impact with her viewers. She developed an elaborate system to catalog the letters and artwork she received so that she could respond to each sender individually rather than use a generic form letter. Her copious notes also allowed her to keep up a running dialogue with those pen pals who wrote in regularly. "When I was a kid, I only imagined that there was someone who actually did such things, so when my chance came, I did it," she said.

And the fans noticed. One anonymous male admirer posted on an Internet message board, "Peggy was a pretty gal with a jubilant and in-your-face cheerfulness that radiated to everyone who watched her." Because he admired her work on the show so much, he drove two and a half hours to see Nicholson at an event in Bloomington. When she learned how far he had traveled to see her, she told him that he must be crazy. "She thanked me just the same for driving all those miles to discover that she was the same funny and cheerful person in person as she was with all of those kids on her show," he said. "She was precious… always wearing her funky decorated MDA T-shirt and sailor's cap that said 'M.V. Paddlewheel Queen.'"

Those who worked at the station recalled that like the other personalities, Nicholson was very generous with her time when it came to making offsite appearances. She never tired of entertaining the crowds at the grand opening of a local supermarket, Market Square Arena or a Muscular Dystrophy Association (MDA) "backyard" carnival. Peggy was always a welcome and very special guest. "She was always volunteered for things around the studio to make herself more valuable," said Reynolds. "She volunteered for Russ and I to go to high school basketball games to

Left: An early autograph card for *Peggy's World*, circa 1975. The show would later be renamed *Popeye & Peggy*. *Courtesy of Peggy Powis.*

Below: An example of artwork that was sent into the WTTV-4 kiddie shows. Peggy catalogued letters and artwork so that she could personally acknowledge fans for their efforts. *Courtesy of Peggy Powis.*

shoot footage to use later, and everyone always recognized her. She was always dragging us into something or other, but it was always fun!"

WORKING WITH RONALD

Nicholson said that she thrived on the personal appearances that allowed her to use the improvisational skills that she had learned in her theater classes in order to make each event special for the kids in attendance. She said some of her favorite events allowed her to appear alongside Indiana's own Ronald McDonald, Don Barnes, an incredible spirit who touched her understanding of what it meant to be a star. "It was always wonderful to get an assignment with McDonald's when I knew he would be there because it was always more fun than work," she noted.

Looking back on those meet-and-greets, Nicholson said, as the second most recognizable character next to Santa Claus, Barnes could have had a star complex, but he never did. She recalled that he was easy to work with and was more than generous with the spotlight. "At every stop, kids would come running to be with him, and he was ever so charming, gentle and genuine with them. But every chance he had, he took my arm and introduced me to the crowds around him like I was the best thing since sliced bread."

Barnes's spirit of generosity was evident when he was out of the makeup as well. Nicholson said that in the three years she worked with him as a member of WTTV, she never saw Barnes out of costume. However, during an MDA event for patients around Halloween, Barnes was in attendance dressed as Groucho Marx and doing magic tricks for the kids. Nicholson thought there was something familiar about the guy, but it wasn't until the MDA executive director revealed his identity that she realized it was her old pal. "I have loved him from the very first time we met, and to this day, he is among my most cherished and beloved friends," she said.

After WTTV phased out *Peggy & Popeye*, Nicholson became the producer of special projects and promotion manager at the station. In that role, she worked closely with the sales department, as well as with president of the Promotion Company Bruce Hubley, who was responsible for bringing several events to the city, including the Ringling Brothers Circus, Holiday on Ice, the Ice Capades, the World's Toughest Rodeo and the Car Craft Street Machine Nationals. The collaboration was so successful that Hubley offered

Volume IV   Number 3   August 12, 1977

MUSCULAR DYSTROPHY ASSOCIATION, INC.

Peggy makes an appearance at an MDA "backyard" carnival, where she greeted fans and often worked with Ronald McDonald (aka Don Barnes). *Courtesy of Peggy Powis.*

Peggy Nicholson with Lenny Elmore on the set of the *Peggy & Popeye* show. *Courtesy of Peggy Powis.*

An ad for the *Popeye & Peggy* show on WTTV-4. Nicholson would be one of the last kiddie hosts on WTTV. *Courtesy of Peggy Powis.*

Nicholson the position of vice-president of the company, and she happily accepted. Little did she know that the partnership would lead to her next "vantastic" television adventure.

PEGGY AND THE VANTASTICS

During her stint at the Promotion Company, Nicholson served as a negotiation companion for KISS 99 radio disc jockey Adam "Smash" Smasher. Smasher was being courted by WTHR-TV Channel 13's general manager Chris Duffy for a children's travelogue show in which Smash and a group of kids would travel to various areas of the city and state learning new things. Smasher had recently left the radio station and was under a non-compete clause for one year. The television show wasn't what he had in mind. As negotiations fell through, Duffy turned to Nicholson and asked, "So, what are YOU doing these days?"

Nicholson demurred, pleased to have been offered another shot at stardom but assuring Duffy that she was happy with her big title at a small company. She returned to her office only to receive a phone call from the **WTHR** programming director pressing her to reconsider. She thanked them but politely declined, insisting that she wasn't interested in another show. When asked what it would take to change her mind, Nicholson put together a list of what she thought was impossible requests only hear back from the station twenty minutes later. They'd agreed to everything. "When can you start?" the programming director asked. *Peggy and the Vantastics* was ready to roll!

Peggy and the Vantastics was designed to appeal to the curious child in everyone. Nicholson played the owner of a fix-it shop (which she rented from a puppet), and each week, she and a group of young friends piled into the Vantastic van to embark on a variety of fun-filled educational adventures that included a tour of the Louisville Slugger baseball-bat factory, a ride in a hot-air balloon and sailing down the Wabash River in a gondola.

The young stars were culled from a series of citywide auditions held at various McDonald's restaurants or recruited on location from the communities in which Nicholson taped her travels. "The *Vantastics* offered the kids who participated in the show an experience of how movies are made," she said. "We shot the same scene several times, often feeding the youngsters lines or making them repeat questions they had asked. The 'live' segments came together on the editing deck, the handy work of many creative editors over the years."

Nicholson said the Vantastics may have carried her name, but it was not her concept. She said her parts were secondary to the brilliant work of Tom Fix, Dave Garrison, Patty Gary and Gene Markiewitz, among others. "The cast of K-I-D-S TV [all puppets] and the characters Wally and Clyde and Bolts were the real stars that earned us recognition from the Indianapolis Education Association. Dave had created another show entitled *This Side Up*, as well as a puppet named Dudley for Channel 13. His work was head and shoulders above anything anyone else was doing creatively," she said, noting that the segments with the puppets were taped when she was not on the set. She was as surprised as everyone else to see how the footage was edited into the show. "They made me look good."

Before parking the van for good three years later, Nicholson began her own company, Peggy Nicholson Marketing, Inc., and secured clients such as the Children's Museum of Indianapolis, the Columbus Indiana Convention and Visitor's Bureau and the Indiana Sports Corporation. She also handled the marketing for a new UHF station that began telecasting on February 1,

An autograph card from Peggy Nicholson's second local show, *Peggy and the Vantastics*, on WTHR-13. *Courtesy of Peggy Powis.*

1984. It was a station that ultimately became a major force in the Indianapolis television market and would lead Nicholson to her third television show, *Peggy's 59er Diner*.

Indy's "new" independent station, WPDS-TV Channel 59, wasn't really new at all. Sarkes Tarzian, who launched WTTV, secured the Channel 59 frequency for the Lafayette market in 1953 as CBS affiliate WFAM-TV before moving it to Channel 18 in 1957. After abandoning the Channel 59 frequency, it remained inactive until it was assigned to the Indianapolis market, where it was resurrected as WPDS in the early '80s.

WPDS-59 originated as a locally owned and operated station that promised a full lineup of programs including cartoons, movies, old sitcoms

Something's always cooking ....

In the late '80s, Peggy Nicholson was the host of *Peggy's 59-er Diner* on the new Indianapolis station WPDS (later WXIN-59). *Courtesy of Peggy Powis.*

and even a nightly newscast. Financed by ANACOMP, the call letters for the new station stood for its three founders: businessman Ron Palamara, former WTHR-13 vice-president Chris Duffy and shopping mall magnate Mel Simon. Duffy approached Nicholson's company to head up the promotion department for the new station, and Nicholson considered it an honor to be among those chosen to launch and manage the new station.

Duffy also knew that having a children's show as part of the new channel's programming was an absolute must, and he already had a seasoned professional on staff with plenty of on-air experience and a built-in fan base. What could be better than asking Nicholson to reprise her on-screen persona? "Hence the *59er Diner*," she said. "*Peggy's 59er Diner* had Chris Duffy's marks all over it, and it was a year of fun, spending time with kids on location, wraps in the studio, etc."

The new show allowed Nicholson the opportunity to reunite with Don Barnes, who shared the show with her, as well as WTTV dynamo Reynolds, who ran her puppet pal Chef Choufleur (along with Rachel Rutledge). "Chef still lives in his denim bag in my attic, and I pulled him out for a Halloween decoration one year," she said. "When the CEO of ANACOMP passed away, the company relocated to California, and the *59er Diner* was cancelled."

In 1985, WPDS was sold to Outlet Broadcasting, which changed the call sign to WXIN. One year later, Channel 59 became a Fox affiliate and was ultimately purchased by Tribune Broadcasting. By the time her third show had ended, Nicholson realized that she had been on and off the air for a total of ten years.

During her stint in television, she continued to be involved in promotions. While working with the White River Park State Games, she met and ultimately fell in love with Rick Powis, a district manager for Hook's Drugs. The two were married in 1985 and eventually settled on Maine's Boothbay Peninsula in 2000.

Peggy's New World

Once she was no longer on TV, Powis realized that she always thought in terms of programming and new ways to use videography. While at the Riley Memorial Association, she shot, directed and edited several developmental pieces and recruitment videos for the campers and counselors at Camp Riley. She also shot footage of her in-laws fiftieth wedding anniversary on VHS. She had to rent studio time in order to edit the piece, traveling back to Indianapolis to work with Bill McKenna at Channel 40 for the project. "About nine years ago…I caught the bug again. I came home and told Rick that I thought I wanted to get back into some video work," she said.

She had to learn new processes and equipment, but she now specializes in projects for nonprofit organizations and claims the Boothbay Region Land Trust and the Boothbay Region Art Foundation as two happy repeat clients. "We have recently filed our DBA papers claiming our business as 'cultural and legacy videography, specializing in packaging documentaries and events for broadcast, Internet and individual distribution,'" she noted.

In recent years, Powis produced an hour-long special for Whitefield, Maine's 200th anniversary entitled *A Remnant in Your Midst: The Irish Catholic*

Spirit in the History of Whitefield, Maine, capturing interviews with active older adults (a lighthouse keeper, woodworkers, authors, historian and castle resident, puzzle people, model train enthusiast, etc.) at St. Andrews Village in Boothbay Harbor. Other productions have included the dedication of a Memorial Day tribute to Samples Shipyard in Boothbay Harbor, the Maine Photography Show and smaller pieces of events on the peninsula, such as the Gingerbread Spectacular.

Still, Powis looks back on her days at Channel 4 as a special part of her career development and hopes to continue working on projects that she loves. She credits the station for giving her the opportunity to stretch creatively and affording her a career that brought a measure of celebrity along with an incredible education. "Our bosses at WTTV must have caught that entrepreneurial spirit for innovation, all the while trusting that those they had hired would carry it out," she said. "It was the best kind of mentoring for those of us who were lucky enough to work there."

CHAPTER 7

A 24/7 Problem

Sometimes it's so easy, I'm ashamed of myself.
—You Can't Do That on Television

By the early 1970s, locally produced kiddie show cavalcades were all but obsolete. Once found in every city and with every turn of the television dial, campy cowboys, ghouls and faux family members were a dying breed. "Very few local shows survived beyond 1973, and the ones that did were often so sanitized and regulated that they resembled their longtime formats in name only," said Hollis. He noted that Buckskin Bill was still on the air in Baton Rouge, Louisiana, in the mid-nineties, but no one pretended that Bill Black was anything other than a regular man in a fringed outfit appearing on location "from whatever local environment seemed to have potential for filling up a half hour."

The television landscape had changed, and viewers' needs changed with it. The FCC regulations caused local stations to move away from the hosted-show format when their "stars" could no longer hawk a sponsor's product on the air. Independents also faced stiff competition from more educational-based programming coming from the federally funded Public Broadcasting System (PBS).

COME AND PLAY

In 1969, after two years of intense research and a combined $8 million grant from the Carnegie Foundation, Ford Foundation and the U.S. government, the Children's Television Workshop began broadcasting *Sesame Street*. It was an innovative and ambitious approach to children's programming that would go on to be the most successful national children's program of all time. Developed in 1966 by Joan Ganz Cooney and featuring the talents of master "muppeteer" Jim Henson, the show introduced children to iconic characters such as Big Bird, Kermit the Frog and Cookie Monster in a cleverly located urban setting. "I remember the first time I ever saw it," said Sonia Manzano, who has portrayed Maria on *Sesame Street* since 1971. In a 2004 interview with the archive of American Television, Manzano said that she was a student at Carnegie Melon University when she saw the show in the student union, mesmerized as James Earl Jones enunciated the alphabet as letters flashed over his head. "It was just so in-your-face and so compelling—it just grabbed me." She was also drawn to the diversity of characters, as well as the city setting that resonated more with her than the suburban images showcased on shows such as *Leave It to Beaver* and *Father Knows Best*. "I saw Susan and Gordon on the stoop, and I thought, 'Hey, that's my street!'" she recalled.

At the beginning of *Sesame Street*'s third season, Manzano was called in for an audition. With two seasons under its belt and having already been satirized on *Saturday Night Live* and *The Tonight Show with Johnny Carson*, she assumed it would not be on the air much longer. She was in for a surprise. Over the next forty years, *Sesame Street* would become a second home for viewers, as well as Manzano, whose character married Luis (played by Emilio Delgado). She gave birth to daughter Gabby while working in the neighborhood fix-it shop.

Sesame Street was only the beginning for innovative programming that would penetrate the PBS landscape. *Mister Rogers' Neighborhood*, starring Fred Rogers, began airing in 1969, followed by *The Electric Company* in 1971. A decade later, *3-2-1 Contact* arrived in 1981, with *Reading Rainbow* hot on its heels in 1983. While these commercial-free shows offered plenty of educational value, there were kids who preferred less pedagogy and personality and more pure programming—twenty-four hours a day if at all possible.

In 1979, those prayers were answered in the form of Nickelodeon, an American cable network show designed to offer a constant stream of commercial-free children's programming. In the ensuing years, it would become the Mecca of kid-centered television channels. "Nickelodeon killed us," Bob Glaze remembered.

NICKELODEON

It may not have "killed" local kiddie shows, but it certainly helped drive another nail in the coffin of the dying art form. Nickelodeon began in 1977 as *Pinwheel* on Columbus, Ohio's QUBE, the first two-way interactive cable television system in the country. QUBE was owned by Warner Cable, which offered the Pinwheel Network as a specialized channel in its cable lineup. With hours of educational programs coming out of the Canadian market, as well as some of the lesser-known regions of the United States, *Pinwheel* appealed to fans of *Sesame Street* and other PBS programs.

Two years later, the all-kids channel was renamed Nickelodeon and relaunched on April 1, 1979, on a number of Warner Cable systems on the East Coast before making its way westward and gaining national prominence. Though it was in the beginning and nowhere near the juggernaut it would eventually become, Nickelodeon was an anomaly because it offered twelve straight hours of commercial-free shows each day. Mornings were dominated by *Pinwheel*, which slowly established itself as a formidable competitor to PBS, while afternoons were geared more for the older viewer, with *What Will They Think of Next?*, *Kids Writes*, *The Third Eye* and the network's breakout slime-spilling hit *You Can't Do That on Television*.

You Can't Do That on Television was designed to be a teenage sendup of the old Rowan & Martin sketch comedy *Laugh In* and featured sixteen-year-old Ottawa, Canada, native Christine McGlade as the show's host. McGlade was discovered when producer Roger Price visited her high school in search of talent for his new production. He was drawn to McGlade's youthful looks and sarcastic personality and quickly hired her for the job.

In a recent interview, McGlade recalled that *You Can't Do That on Television* was much more popular in the United States than it was in Canada. "We never had the same degree of success in Canada as we did in the United States. For me, it was always a bit of a shock to travel in the States and be recognized in airports and malls."

Anderson, Indiana, native Fred Newman also got his big break on the new network as the host of the teenage talk show *Livewire*. In 1983, *People* magazine wrote that Newman combined the candor of Phil Donahue with the wacky wit of Steve Martin to win "the hearts of that most elusive of television audiences, the 12-to-15-year-olds." It was a formula that would work more than once in his career, as he strove to stay tapped into what kids wanted from their television programming.

While some new stars were being culled from the new network, veteran TV personality Don Herbert's (aka Mr. Wizard) career was reinvigorated when Nickelodeon came calling. *Watch Mr. Wizard* originally aired on NBC from 1951–65, with Herbert showcasing a number of scientific concepts and lab experiments. The show was revamped for the Canadian market in 1971 as *Mr. Wizard* but failed to catch on. When Nickelodeon offered Herbert the chance to create a faster-paced version of the show for the cable channel, he agreed to appear three times a week. During its run, it was the number-three show on the network behind *You Can't Do That on Television* and *Livewire*. It was a rare case of a vintage host making the shift to more modern-day, cable-based television.

But for all of its early success, like the kiddie shows that came before it, Nickelodeon had its share of problems and growing pains. By 1984, the network had lost $10 million and lacked a solid lineup of successful shows. The solution was to change management companies and give Nickelodeon an MTV-style makeover by taking on advertisers and incorporating commercials within the programming day. Within six months of that rebranding, Nickelodeon became the dominant channel in children's programming and has remained so ever since.

The Disney Channel

With the advent of cable television, it was only a matter of time before Walt Disney Productions started exploring options within the new broadcast medium. The first discussions about bringing an entire channel devoted to Disney programming to cable began in 1977. The idea was summarily dismissed. Five years later, Disney revisited the idea and began to turn the dream of a Disney-dedicated network into a reality. The result was the Disney Channel.

Launched on April 18, 1983, as a premium offering on cable systems, the Disney Channel carried an array of original commercial-free programming, including *Welcome to Pooh Corner* and *You and Me Kid*, along with imported animated series, vintage Disney material and featured re-runs of old favorites such as *The Adventures of Ozzie and Harriet* and *The Mickey Mouse Club*.

Like Nickelodeon, the Disney Channel saw the logic in not only offering original shows but also revamping proven programming. In 1989, Disney reconfigured *The Mickey Mouse Club* with an updated image and a new cast while keeping some of the winning formula from the old format. It wasn't the first time that Disney had updated its premier kiddie show—in the 1970s, it debuted *The All-New Mickey Mouse Club*, which featured a disco-era theme song and a more ethnically diverse cast compared to the 1950s version. One of the new cast members included Lisa Welchel, who would go on to play Blair Warner for nine years on *The Facts of Life*.

According to a 1999 article in the *Orlando Sentinel*, more than five thousand kids showed up to audition for *The All-New Mickey Mouse Club*'s opening season, and once it was proven to be a hit, more than twenty thousand young hopefuls auditioned for the following season. "They knew they were auditioning for this hot show that was great to get on," said Steve Clements, executive producer of the show.

The All-New Mickey Mouse Club (later shortened to *MMC*) featured many of the elements that had made the show so successful in the past. Serials, theme days, music and dancing were all hallmarks of the new version of the show; however, one of the club's most notable trademarks was missing: the mouse ears. Executives decided that the new cast of the *MMC* would don high-school Mouseketeer jackets instead.

Disney scored big when they hired *Livewire*'s Fred Newman to lead the club through its first six seasons. They knew that he had a seemingly limitless supply of character personalities and voices, but he was also a familiar face and the kind of adult kids and teens related to. "I was leery of getting involved with a show that many people remember for the Mouseketeers and that 'Gee whiz, kids' attitude," Newman told the *Palm Beach Post* in 1989. However, he relaxed when he saw that the channel was trying to take the successful show and move it into a more updated and relevant format for the early-nineties viewer.

Just as the original *Mickey Mouse Club* launched the successful careers of some of its members, such as Annette Funicello, the *MMC* was the first stop on the road to superstardom for then-unknown Mouseketeers Justin Timberlake, Britney Spears, Christina Aguilera and Keri Russell.

Tony Lucca was part of the *MMC* from 1991 to 1995. A member of the Emerald Cove serial, as well the *MMC*'s pop singing group that traveled

Tony Lucca of the Disney Channel's *All-New Mickey Mouse Club* and author Julie Young in 1993. The show later launched the careers of Britney Spears, Keri Russell and Justin Timberlake but helped end an era of locally produced children's programming. *Author's private collection.*

Members of the Disney Channel's *All-New Mickey Mouse Club* (later the *MMC*) perform at the old Target center in Greenwood. *Author's private collection.*

across country performing in front of their fans to promote the show, Luca said that the club was an incredible family that he was lucky to be part of. "To call it a club, I think, undersells how intense the relationships were that we formed so long ago, as well as the talent," he said in an NBC *Today Show* interview while competing on *The Voice* (where he was reunited with fellow *MMC* star Aguilera). "It's always been amazing when another [success] story unfolds."

The Disney Channel quickly established itself as the gold standard for quality programming and family entertainment, and over the years, the channel has continually worked to offer the best shows it can. Now part of the basic cable package, the channel has had to eschew their commercial-free format; however, its "commercials" tend to focus on programming previews, video releases or other Disney promotions. By 2002, the Disney Channel was seen in 80 million homes nationwide and has brought the public many beloved shows, including *Hannah Montana*, *That's So Raven*, *The Wizards of Waverly Place* and *The Suite Life of Zack and Cody*.

While other children's channels continue to gear their primetime shows to an adult or family audience (ala Nick at Nite), the Disney Channel is the only network that is completely devoted to kids' programming twenty-four hours a day. Based on the history of its parent company, it's assured that the "house of mouse" network will continue to grow and evolve to meet the needs of its audience.

THE CARTOON NETWORK

On October 1, 1992, a new channel crept into the cable lineup. The aptly named Cartoon Network promised a 24/7 offering of classic animation that was at the heart and soul of locally produced children's shows.

Owned by Turner Broadcasting mogul Ted Turner, the Cartoon Network boasted the old MGM cartoon catalogue, which included the pre-1948 color *Looney Tunes* shorts and the *Merrie Melodies* library, the Fleischer Studios Popeye cartoons and even the Hanna-Barbera catalogue.

It seemed like a tall order—after all, what parent would let their child watch nothing but cartoons all day? Still, Turner had experience with making the impossible possible. When scoffers said that no viewer would tolerate a network devoted to nothing but the news, Turner proved them wrong with CNN and CNN Headline News. Why would a cartoon network be any different? There was more than enough material to fill a day's worth of programming, but there were problems breaking into existing cable systems. Turner finally decided to bundle the new network with some of his solid performers, such as WTBS and TNT. Within a few short years, the Cartoon Network built its ratings and by 1994 was enjoying its place as the fifth most popular cable channel in the United States.

The Cartoon Network has taken its share of hits over the years. What started as a vehicle to rerun old classics was soon giving life to some of the latest and greatest in animated concepts. Shows such as *The Powerpuff Girls*, *Johnny Bravo* and *Dexter's Laboratory* proved to be big hits, while critics have suggested that other efforts display a lack of imagination.

The addition of the Adult Swim block offered grownups the chance to enjoy cartoons with more mature content (including the much ballyhooed *Boondocks* series), while the annual Bugs Bunny marathon was panned for showcasing cartoons with politically incorrect messages. However, the inclusion of reality shows in the "all-cartoon" lineup has rankled some viewers who felt the channel had departed from its original concept. "Gone are the days of *The Powerpuff Girls*, *Dexter's Laboratory* and Cartoon Cartoon Fridays. Now we have quiz shows on roller coasters, pint-sized ghost hunters and a *Survivor* rip-off," said blogger Tim Surette. "It's a little sad," said Craig McCracken, creator of *The Powerpuff Girls*, in an *LA Times* interview. "Cartoon Network had something really unique."

Fade to Black

In his article "Local Kid's Shows Gone But Not Forgotten," journalist Brian Daley noted that the disappearance of local celebrities is one of the many unforeseen consequences in the evolution of the modern media. Daley wrote, "As newspapers fold, radio stations turn to syndication, and television continues to add cable networks, the mere concept of the local celebrity seems hard to imagine." The Kids TV program host has become extinct in a world in which channels such as Nickelodeon, the Cartoon Network and the Disney Channel can run hours upon hours of cartoons and other programs without giving its viewers a face to connect with. Daley wondered if standardized programming throughout the nation denoted a loss of local identity. "Sponge Bob could never have convinced me to run out and buy a jar of Bosco, but Captain Satellite sure could," he wrote. "We never could have done the kind of shows we did in the cable era with competitors like Nickelodeon out there," Janie Hodge said. "We were lucky to come about when we did."

If the inception of 24/7 kids' networks didn't bury the local cartoon show or independent station personality, a shift in ownership did. If an independent station was sold or a new station manager was brought in to revamp the lineup, it didn't take long for the pink slips to fly. Mark Carter recalls, "My father's show was cancelled several times over the years, but I do remember the day he got that final call after the station had been sold and him jumping up from the table in order to run down and salvage every Sammy Terry set piece and prop he could before they were destroyed."

However, if the golden era of WTTV-4 personalities was on the decline, the station was determined to create one last memorable character before fading to black once and for all.

CHAPTER 8

Commander KC

In 1990, the United States Congress passed the Children's Television Act, which, along with subsequent rules adopted by the Federal Communications Commission, was designed to increase the level of educational and informational programming for children available on television. Not only was the act geared to limit the amount of time stations devoted to advertisements during children's programs, but it also prohibited "program talent or other identifiable program characteristics to deliver commercials during or adjacent to children's programming featuring that character."

This act (and its variations in prior years) was a huge blow to stations that used their on-air personalities as pitchmen and pitchwomen for a sponsor's product. By the mid-eighties, *Cowboy Bob's Corral* and the *Janie* show were cancelled, leaving Sammy Terry the lone character host on WTTV's lineup. The station still ran blocks of cartoons before and after school, but there was no economic advantage to develop an entire show around a specific personality. However, there was a need to give young viewers a "face" with whom they could connect. Enter Commander KC.

Commander KC was designed to be the leader of the Channel 4 Kids Club, and while not a traditional cartoon host or product pitchman, she was a station ambassador charged with bringing educational and informative vignettes (sponsored by WTTV advertisers) between cartoon programs.

According to Mindy Winkler, who served as Commander KC from 2001–02, the $2 million Kids Club campaign was a solid part of the station's revenue. "There was this theory that kids couldn't differentiate between a commercial and a cartoon, and in order to offer something less influential, our vignettes were designed to focus more on the sponsor's message rather than the sponsor itself," she said.

While Commander KC could not endorse a specific product or organization, she could offer fun animal facts that were brought to viewers courtesy of the Indianapolis Zoo. She could also talk about historical events and the benefits of exercise thanks to Conner Prairie Interactive History Park or the Greater Indianapolis YMCA.

But that was only part of it. The Kids Club also enabled sponsors to connect with their targeted audience through birthday greetings, the club newsletter and special events that featured Commander KC herself. "Sponsors gave us a ton of promotional materials to stuff into our goody bags, which went directly into the hands of the kids and their parents," Winkler said.

Commander I and II

The WTTV-4 Kids Club campaign kicked off with perky Cindy Goodwin in the bright red, military-style Commander KC uniform. Though she was only in command a short time before moving on to other opportunities, colleagues said she helped establish the Kids Club and its persona for the station and gave the promotion a sturdy foundation.

Staci Edwards interned under Goodwin's Commander KC and said that the first Kids Club meetings took place in local McDonald's restaurants until a sponsorship change switched club headquarters to Dairy Queen. Edwards said that Goodwin held the Commander KC position for two years prior to leaving the station, and although there have been a number of rumors as to why she left, it was not as dramatic as everyone made it out to be. "She had other things she wanted to do, and that was that," Edwards said.

After Goodwin's departure in 1993, the station immediately sought to find a new Commander. Perry Meridian High School graduate Edwards said that she had no drama experience and no aspirations of being an on-air personality when it was suggested that she audition for the coveted role. She had a degree in organization communications from Indiana University and was content in her position as a marketing and promotions person but ultimately decided to try out for the job. "Because I had been one of Cindy's interns, I saw everything that went along with the job, so I figured, why not?" she recalled.

Commander KC (aka Cindy Goodwin) poses with Chris Young at a Castleton Square event sponsored by the Disney Store. Goodwin was the first person to sport Commander KC's red jacket. *Author's private collection.*

To her surprise, she got the job and assumed her new role with enthusiasm, promising her father not to let the celebrity status go to her head. Upon receiving her red blazer, Edwards worked with a local badge company to create a new Commander KC insignia that had less of a military appearance and would be more fun for the young viewers. It was also suggested that she visit a hairstylist who had some experience with television personalities to create a look for the new leader of the club. The result was not quite what she had in mind. "They dyed my hair red," Edwards said, laughing at the ill-fated follicle experiment. "I'm a brunette, and while I have some auburn in my hair, it's not red. I tried it, but ultimately I let it grow out and went with my natural color."

Because the name "Commander KC" came with a certain amount of ambiguity, the station made no formal on-air announcement about the cast change. Edwards assumed that the station was hoping for a seamless transition, and although there was an announcement in the *Indianapolis Star* heralding the new Channel 4 star, the young viewers weren't prepared for the switch. They were skeptical when they first met Edwards at those initial public appearances and often asked where was the "other" commander. "I understood that they didn't want to make a big deal about it, but it would have been helpful to have some announcement about the change, especially for the kids' sake," she said.

Staci Edwards became the second and longest-running Commander KC for WTTV-4 in 1993. *Courtesy of Staci Edwards.*

Throughout the week, Edwards wrote and filmed her vignettes, penned the Kids Club newsletter, signed birthday cards, accompanied the sales staff on calls for new sponsors and brought her live show to schools throughout central Indiana. Working with the Indiana Pacers mascot Boomer, Edwards brought a high-energy show that allowed her to expand her sponsors' messages and get the kids on their feet. She said Boomer was the perfect partner for her live shows because he could dazzle the kids with his stunts while she served as the silent mascot's voice.

Personal appearances were another big component of being Commander KC, and there were few weekends during which she wasn't expected to appear at a Kids Club meeting at Dairy Queen, the state fairgrounds, Colts games or a myriad of other locations. But Edwards said she never tired of greeting the kids, signing autographs or posing for a picture—even if it was when she was shopping in Venture at 10:00 p.m. and was spotted by an overenthusiastic family who recognized her sans blazer and makeup. "I don't know how they spotted me sometimes," she laughed. "I would have thought I was unrecognizable, but I guess not. I'd hear 'Hey look, it's Commander KC!'"

Edwards said that portraying Commander KC for nearly eight years not only made her a celebrity throughout the WTTV-4 viewing area but also provided her with opportunities most people never get to enjoy. She said she was able to go behind the scenes at the Indianapolis Zoo, travel to Disney World twice and serve as the guest ringmaster when the Ringling Bros. and Barnum & Bailey Circus came to town. "I got to do things that most people don't get to do in their entire lives!" she said.

During her time with the station, Edwards was able to take part in the fiftieth anniversary celebration in 1999 and compete against "Cowboy Bob" Glaze during the *Hoosier Know-It-Alls* history quiz show. Glaze was a favorite of Edwards' as a kid, and she was nervous about going up against the Channel 4 host that she used to watch. "He won, and I jokingly told him that it was because he had been around longer than I had, but it was a lot of fun to meet him, Sammy Terry, Janie and all of the Channel 4 personalities I remembered," she recalled.

But not every moment on the job was lighthearted. Edwards made many visits to Riley Children's Hospital as Commander KC, touring the units and greeting patients all while trying to stay strong for the kids. She recalled:

I could start tearing up just thinking about the visits to Riley Hospital and seeing kids who didn't deserve to be as sick as they were. Often I would be

Full House star Jodi Sweetin poses with Staci Edwards as Commander KC at an Indianapolis Ice hockey game. *Courtesy of Staci Edwards.*

> *accompanied by the ice cream cone mascot from Dairy Queen, and there were times when I could hear her crying inside the suit, but I knew I couldn't do that. I had to keep it together, because they were counting on me. We did a lot of programming for the Riley kids…it was shot and broadcast through the television studio in the hospital. I really enjoyed visiting them. They would see me and give me the biggest hug like I was a hero to them, but really they were the heroes.*

In 2001, after eight years as the head of the Kids Club, Edwards was ready to hang up her red jacket and start a family with her husband, who she met at WTTV. As it turned out, the end of her run as Commander KC came at a fortuitous time, as her father fell ill and she felt compelled to devote more time to him. "I really credit my boss, Peggy McCelland, for understanding how important that was to me," Edwards said. "And even though they were content to let me stay on as the Commander, she recognized that I needed to be with my dad, who passed away three months later. I had a wonderful family at WTTV…they were there for me during that difficult time."

When her time as Commander KC came to a close, Edwards worked for Emmis Communications and eventually took time off to be with her son before returning to the workplace, first as a volunteer at her son's school and now as an elementary resource tutor. She has recently taken over the closed-circuit television station in the school, and while some of the students and faculty do not know about her "celebrity" past, others do. "I miss working at the station, and at least through the TV studio at school, I am able to revisit that and help students see what it's like to be on the news," she said. "I am very proud of my time there, and I still have the red jacket and the 'Froggy' award we won for one of my vignettes. I still think it was the best job I will ever have and certainly one that provided me with some of the best opportunities I ever had."

COMMANDER III

Like Edwards, Anderson native Mindy Winkler was no stranger to the classic Channel 4 personalities such as Janie, Cowboy Bob and Sammy Terry, as well as others she watched as a kid growing up in the '70s and '80s. But she never dreamed that she would join their ranks or earn the distinction of being the last on-air children's personality before WTTV was sold to a FOX affiliate in 2002.

When Winkler learned that Edwards was leaving her post as Commander KC and that WTTV was looking for a replacement, she jumped at the chance to audition for the role. "I remembered seeing Staci as Commander KC when I was in college, and when I saw the ad for open auditions in the classified section of the paper, I knew it was right up my alley—I had to try out," she said.

A graduate of Ball State University with degrees in broadcast television and information/communication sciences, Winkler had a full-time position at a video hardware company and was keeping busy on the weekends as an Indianapolis Colts cheerleader in 2001 when she saw the ad that changed her life. She sent in her resume along with hundreds of others who all promised to bring the fresh ideas, ebullient personality and Internet experience that the job required. She said the station waded through all of the applicants and narrowed their choice to six finalists who were brought in to audition in front of Peggy McCelland, who was to be instrumental in making the final decision. "I was the last person to audition that day," Winkler recalled. "I came in there, and when they asked me to perform, I broke into this little song I used to sing when I was twelve called 'Kids Were Made for Fun' from *The Runaway Snowman*. It's a great little song, and they thought I wrote it. I felt really good about their reaction, and I suspected that I was going to get the job."

A few weeks later, the station called to confirm her hunch, and after contract negotiations were completed, Winker became the third and ultimately last Commander KC in July 5, 2001, at the age of thirty. Her official title was Community Affairs Liaison, and like Edwards, she hit the ground running in her new role. She said that hundreds of photos were taken for autograph cards, birthday greetings and other promotional materials, which meant she had to find a hairstyle and look she could live with for the duration of her time in the Commander KC jacket. "I am a natural brunette, but I went blond for the Colts, so when it was time to shoot the photos for Commander KC, I was asked if I wanted to go back to brown. At that point, I was used to being blond, so I stuck with it," she said. "Besides, it kind of fits my personality."

The station again downplayed the change in Commanders, and Winkler said she too received skepticism from viewers who were used to seeing Edwards in the role. She said she found it humorous that after seven years of Edwards being the face of Commander KC, the station thought it could roll out someone who looked so markedly different without anyone noticing. "The kids who grew up with Staci weren't fooled," she mused.

Although Winkler wasted no time in making the position of Commander KC her own, it was understood around the station that Commander KC was expected to behave in an appropriate manner whether in uniform or not. She took that message to heart and made sure not to be seen in compromising situations that could dissuade sponsors or make the station look bad in anyway. "I always remembered that I was representing the station at all times."

Winkler's sponsors included, Conner Prairie, the Indianapolis Zoo, the Greater Indianapolis YMCA, the Indianapolis Power & Light Company and Dairy Queen, with whom she worked to create her vignettes, develop a live show and schedule personal appearances. She recalled:

I helped bring in a lot of sponsors, including Mars Music, who supplied the sound for the live show. There were a variety of sponsorship levels that advertisers could choose from. Some of them placed ads in the newsletter, while

A WB4 Kids Club birthday card featuring Commander KC was sent to members and contained freebies from WTTV-4 sponsors. *Courtesy of Staci Edwards.*

others lent their names to live events or on-air promotions. Still others supplied coupons that were placed inside WTTV Kids Club birthday cards.

The station was adamant that coupons included in the birthday greetings gave the viewer something for free, whether that was a Dilly Bar at Dairy Queen or a free admission to Conner Prairie. Winkler said it couldn't be a "BOGO" (buy one, get one) deal, and while some businesses were quick to see the marketing potential, others did not. "They just didn't understand that if you give the birthday kid something for free, the parents and the family would have to bring them out to redeem the coupon," she laughed.

"We had over 100,000 names in that database, so companies were sure to get additional sales out of giving something away for free."

As a Colts cheerleader, Winkler was used to spending the occasional weekend away from home making appearances with other members of the squad, but as Commander KC, she said there was a festival or parade nearly every Saturday and Sunday. Unlike sharing the spotlight with three other people, she said it was surreal to be the focus of everyone in attendance. Still, she loved meeting the kids, posing for pictures and signing autographs, especially when she was able to see old friends who now brought their kids to say hello.

Not only did she put in seventy to eighty hours a week as her alter ego both in and outside of the studio, but during the summer, Winkler spent eight hours a day at the Indiana State Fair passing out goody bags and visiting with the fans. "I was constantly stuffing goody bags at my home, at the station, everywhere," she said. "I had interns working with me to stuff them. I had my family sitting around stuffing them." There were also a number of contests associated with the Kids Club, which kept Winkler and the other Commanders hopping with entries and prize giveaways. She said that it didn't matter if it was two tickets to Conner Prairie or another nominal award; she was always deluged with thousands of postcards from kids trying to win.

But rest assured—someone always won. Winkler said that she often wondered if the contests she heard about at WTTV when she was a kid were really legitimate, but as Commander KC, she knew for a fact that they were. Such was the case when she donated an appearance in one of her vignettes to a silent auction. The winners were two young boys who dressed up as the Blues Brothers and danced with Winkler during what became one of her most popular on-air spots. "It made them pretty famous around their school," she said. "Being Commander KC was surreal, but it was so much fun. It never felt like work."

One of the more surreal moments occurred on September 11, 2001, when she arrived at WISH-TV 8 for a meeting of all of the local community affairs liaisons and learned of the terrorist attacks at the World Trade Center and the Pentagon. "The meeting was cancelled of course, but I didn't know that when I walked in. Still, it was wild to be in a news station while all of that was going on. Everyone was running everywhere, and when I got back to Channel 4, I had to show four pieces of ID."

The following weekend, there was a taping of the *Hoosier Millionaire* show in Winkler's hometown of Anderson, and prior to the start of the game,

Above: Commander KC Staci Edwards greets her fans at the Indianapolis Motor Speedway. *Courtesy of Staci Edwards.*

Left: The WB4 *Dubba* newsletter that was sent to members of the WB4 Kids' Club and featured Commander KC. *Author's private collection.*

she was asked to take the stage and lead the crowd in singing "God Bless America" while wearing her Commander KC uniform. She said it was incredible to be in television during such a seminal moment in U.S. history.

In 2002, when the station was sold, Commander KC and the Kids Club relocated to a new studio. However, it wasn't long before the station decided to discontinue the campaign. Winkler said she was surprised that it came to an abrupt end, considering its popularity, but she reluctantly shrugged off her blazer and turned in her epaulets. "I didn't even get to keep the jacket," she said sadly.

After leaving Channel 4, Winkler reconfigured the Kids Club live show and rechristened it the *Mindy and the Fun Company*. As the leader of the showcase, Winkler chooses the music, writes alternative lyrics to popular songs and serves as the lead singer of the show. She said that schools happily accepted her sans the Commander KC personality and that they love her anti-drug/anti-bullying/anti-tobacco message, which still offers the students a chance to have fun. She has also segued into radio, serving as the traffic reporter for Z99.5 FM, 104.5 WJJK FM, 102.5 WMDH and Freedom 95.9. She also has her own television show on WTHR-13, a webcast called "Mindy's Mixers," and is constantly seeking out new opportunities. "I've never forgotten how lucky I was to represent WTTV-4, and I still have people who recognize me as Commander KC," she said. "It was the greatest job in the world, and I would have done it until I was ninety-two!"

CHAPTER 9

Stay Tuned

Stay tuned—we'll be right back!
—children's television hosts everywhere

T hree years ago, I wrote a simple blog post that paid tribute to one of my childhood television heroes. I never dreamed that it would lead to an online friendship with that very person, a magazine article or an entire book. What started as a simple idea to round up some of the old WTTV-4 personalities, interview them and share their stories with the masses turned into a much more complex proposition. As I began researching material for this book, I realized that the evolution of local children's television programming and its place in pop culture history is not a short subject. I have no doubt that volumes could be written about this subject and that I was limited on the amount of information I could offer in this space.

AN INCREDIBLE OPPORTUNITY

Writing this book brought me in touch with some very dear people who meant so much to me as a child and even more as an adult. Peggy (Nicholson) Powis has become like an extended member of my family. Her periodic e-mails read as though we spoke just a few days ago when, in some cases,

Cowboy Bob Glaze performs at the Irving Theater in Indianapolis. *Author's private collection.*

Author Julie Young and Janie Hodge in Lawrence, Indiana, February 2011. *Author's private collection.*

Sammy Terry (aka Mark Carter) and author Julie Young at the Children's Museum of Indianapolis in October 2012. *Author's private collection.*

weeks and months have gone by. Though we have not seen each other face to face since 1975, we have exchanged photos. She still looks the same, and she assures me that I do as well. While that's highly unlikely, it's so wonderful that Peggy's personal touch still shines through and that she still believes in keeping a little of the television magic alive with those who watched her. She truly is "vantastic!"

I was at the Irving Theater event in the Indianapolis neighborhood of Irvington in November 2010 when Harlow Hickenlopper (aka Hal Fryer, who appeared on WTHR and later hosted the morning programming on WFYI-20), Cowboy Bob and Janie entertained hundreds of fans who turned out to revisit the memories of their childhoods. Cowboy Bob went into his trademark shtick with corny jokes and funny stories, while Janie mesmerized the room full of adults by reading "The Night Before Christmas" and singing "If You're Happy and You Know It." (Yes, we all clapped our hands and sang along!)

I visited with Janie over a couple of meals and found her to be a delightful woman who generously answered my questions with a grace and class I can only hope to emulate. I spent an afternoon with Bob Glaze at his Morgantown home, where I found him to be exactly like his onscreen persona. As we said goodbye after our interview, I remember thanking him for being a constant presence in my life for so many years, for teaching me to "Stop, Drop and Roll" and for all of the music and laughs. He still seems genuinely touched to learn that his little cartoon show meant so much to so many.

I even had the chance to hang out in Sammy Terry's dungeon and tag along with Indy's favorite ghoul at a personal appearance at the Children's Museum. Though I was not able to interview Bob Carter for this book, I learned that I had met the man behind the cowl a number of times at the Family Music Center on Shadeland Avenue, never knowing that the nice older man who helped me select sheet music was none other than Sammy Terry himself! (It's probably all for the best. If I had known, it's unlikely that my parents would have gotten me out of the music store!) I was able to share my Sammy Terry experiences with my youngest son, who even had an unfortunate encounter with Sammy's guillotine but now stays up on Halloween night in order to experience the annual horror show as one of the next generation of Sammy Terry fans.

Other Notable Names

This book also shed some light on the visionary station manager Don Tillman, who left WTTV-4 in 1981 to join KTTV Channel 11 in Los Angeles, where he served as the vice-president of programming and production. According to his online biography, part of Tillman's responsibility at the twelve-acre facility was producing hundreds of national television series, including *All in the Family, Star Search, Family Ties, The Facts of Life, Too Close for Comfort* and *Love Connection*.

Remaining true to his commitment to find and develop local talent, Tillman created Trojan Vision for the University of Southern California (USC) School of Cinematic Arts. Trojan Vision began as a student-run television station with eight students and grew into a 24/7 operation that produces more than 1,900 hours of original programming each semester. Over the years, Tillman has been accorded a number of honors, including four Emmys, a Gold Medal from the International Film Festival, five Angel Awards, three Telly Awards, the Gabriel Award and a Lifetime Achievement Award from the Hollywood Chamber of Commerce for his contribution to the entertainment industry. Don was inducted into the Indiana Broadcasters

Hall of Fame and received a Sagamore of the Wabash, the highest award presented by the governor of the state of Indiana.

Producer Peggy McCelland left WTTV in 1989 to become the production manager for KFVE-TV in Honolulu, Hawaii. Six years later, she returned to Indiana as the executive producer of WNDY but in 1997 made the move back to WTTV, where she developed the Commander KC persona and kept the spirit of a WTTV-4 children's personality alive until 2003. Today, McCelland serves as the executive producer of the *Indy Style* show, which airs weekday mornings on WISH-TV and is planning a memoir of her work in television. "We called each other the 'other' Peggy," said Powis. "It was a privilege to work with her."

Channel 4 was known for programming beyond the kiddie arena, including Jim Gerard's long-running talk show, Frank Edwards's *Stranger than Science*, a UFO/paranormal program that ran in the late 1950s and early '60s and sports offerings that included Indiana University basketball coach Bobby Knight's Sunday showcase and *Championship Wrestling* with commentator Bob Carter.

Known for such names as Dick the Bruiser (William Afflis), Wilbur Snyder and "Cowboy Bob" Ellis, *Championship Wrestling* began in 1964. Before Hulk Hogan and Stone Cold Steve Austin took to the ring for their own brand of performance sports, the brawlers of *Championship Wrestling* were synonymous with WTTV-4 and the rest of the Indiana landscape. I well remember seeing Dick the Bruiser on TV commercials in the 1970s and cringing when my mother told me that the legendary wrestler had asked her out on a date. "Did you go?" I asked, incredulously. His raspy voice and tough-guy personality seemed so off-putting to my six-year-old self. "Are you kidding me?" she replied. "I wouldn't have gotten in a car with him on a bet!" After her death, my uncle confirmed the story and even remembered the restaurant where the proposition occurred. "All of those guys lived around here, so it wasn't that uncommon to run into them in public places," he said.

WHEN A KID COULD BE A KID

And that's what made the local celebrities/television personalities so important—they lived nearby and understood the lay of the land. They looked into the camera and talked about the people and places that mattered to their viewers, and there was always a sense of a shared experience between the host and the kids at home.

Over eighteen months of research went into this book, and in that time, I discovered how lucky I was to have grown up at a time when I was only one generation removed from shows such as *Howdy Doody*, *Roy Rogers* and the original *Mickey Mouse Club*. These were the shows my parents watched when there were only a few channels to choose from and an even smaller cache of broadcast material available. Luckily, I was able to catch most of these black-and-white classics on reruns during various points of my childhood, and I remember it taking me forever to reconcile that the brunette singing "Pretty Is as Pretty Does" on the *Mickey Mouse Club* was the same soccer mom that sent her kids off to school with their Skippy peanut butter sandwiches in the '80s.

It was interesting to learn that my peers and I were the guinea-pig audience for shows that would become PBS staples such as *Sesame Street*, *Mister Rogers' Neighborhood*, *The Electric Company* and *3-2-1 Contact*. Personally, I found *Sesame Street* to be a tad too repetitive, but I loved Cookie Monster, Big Bird and Oscar the Grouch, so occasionally I tuned in. *The Electric Company*'s opening, "Hey you guys!" struck me as jarring, so I skipped that show and *3-2-1 Contact* altogether. But *Mister Rogers*—now that was appointment TV as far as I was concerned. Any grownup who understood the concept of make-believe and had an entire neighborhood devoted to his imagination was the kind of man I wanted living next door to me.

My "wonder years" occurred at the dawn of the cable television era, when the magic box atop the TV offered forty channels of anything and everything imaginable. On a given day, I might see *I Love Lucy*, *The Three Stooges*, *The Bozo Show* out of Chicago and an old *Alvin and the Chipmunks* cartoon before I tuned into my prime time favorites, which included *Mork & Mindy*, *Happy Days* and *The Facts of Life*. Looking back on it, the advent of cable television posed many of the same problems early networks faced when there was too much time and not enough content to go around. I well remember a time when Nickelodeon ended its programming day and the Arts & Entertainment network took over at 8:00 p.m.

I saw *Pinwheel* enough to get its silly theme song stuck in my head, and I still torment my son with it whenever I am feeling particularly whimsical. I learned how to make a toothpaste alternative using everyday ingredients by watching *What Will They Think of Next?* (an experiment that went horribly awry when my mother found the white powdery substance in my bottom desk drawer and did NOT think that it was tooth powder I was hiding in

Staci Edwards looks back fondly on her days as Commander KC. *Author's private collection.*

there). I loved watching the mime troop on *Kids' Writes* act out the letters and stories viewers sent in, and I certainly knew what magic words would cause the slime to fall on "Moose" McGlade and the gang on *You Can't Do That on Television.*

While it seemed that I had a diverse amount of television choices during my formative years, it was nothing compared to what my own children had between Saturday morning shows, Nickelodeon, the Disney Channel, Cartoon Network and an assortment of subsidiary channels too numerous to mention.

But I had something they never did, and that was the local television personalities who came into my living room and ultimately became a part of my very existence. I'm grateful that my eldest son at least had the chance to experience (no matter how briefly) the thrill of having a local personality all of his own in the form of Commander KC, because I well remember putting on my school uniform each day before pouring a bowl of Frosted Flakes as Cowboy Bob invited me to spend some time on the corral. I was able to catch a little of the *Janie* show before my mother switched the channel to Donahue, and of course I never missed Peggy in the afternoons or Sammy Terry on Friday nights.

Tim Hollis noted that in recent years, there has been a push to return to that old style of programming that seemed to work well "either with new talent or by bringing back some of the veteran hosts" but that most of these were doomed from the get go, especially when they tried to put a modern spin on something that is inherently nostalgic.

In an interview with *TV Guide*, Chuck Zink (aka South Florida's "Skipper Chuck") said that the children's television hosts enjoyed a fantastic influence on their viewers with little monetary reimbursement for their efforts, and it's important to recognize their contribution to a time when a kid could be a kid—a time I am profoundly grateful to have been a part of.

Bibliography

Archive of American Television. "Interview with Fred Rogers." http://www.emmytvlegends.org/interviews/people/fred-rogers.

———. "Interview with Sonia Manzano." http://www.emmytvlegends.org/interviews/people/sonia-manzano.

Bellis, Mary. "The Origins of Children's Television Broadcasting." http://inventors.about.com/od/kidactivities/a/children_tv.htm.

Daley, Brian. "Local Kid Shows Gone But Not Forgotten." National Academy of Television Arts & Sciences. http://www.emmysf.tv/articles/380-local-kids-shows-gone-but-not-forgotten.html.

Funicello, Annette. *A Dream Is a Wish Your Heart Makes*. New York: Hyperion Books, 1994.

Gardner, Caine. "Cowboy Bob, Janie on Reunion Trail with CD." Greencastle *Banner Graphic*. December 14, 2007.

Hicks, L. Wayne. "Interview with Bob Keeshan." TVparty.com. http://www.tvparty.com/keeshan1.html.

Hinman, Catherine. "Way Cool Mouseketeers: The Disney Channel's Mickey Mouse Club Is Back in Production with 10 New Stars, a New Co-Host and a Loyal Following." *Orlando Sentinel*. May 31, 1991.

Hollis, Tim. *Hi There, Boys and Girls: America's Local Children's TV Programs.* Jackson: University Press of Mississippi, 2001.

Hunter, Al. "Interview with Cowboy Bob." http://www.youtube.com/watch?v=Zd9l07JyRd4.

———. "Interview with Janie." http://www.youtube.com/watch?v=nMX4LiEKmu0.

Ingram, Billy. *TV Party: Television's Untold Tales.* Los Angeles: Bonus Books, 2002.

Ingram, Billy, and Kevin S. Butler. "Soupy Sales Show." TVparty.com. http://www.tvparty.com/soupy.html.

———. "What Happened to the Our Gang Cast?" TVparty.com. http://www.tvparty.com/50rascals3.html.

Khan, Toby. "By Talking Both Straight and Silly to Teens, Fred Newman Is Cable's Pied Piper of Puberty." *People.* July 4, 1983.

Knight, Dana. "City's Favorite Ghoul Gives Up Day Job." *Indianapolis Star.* July 12, 2001.

Martin, Lara. "The Voice's Tony Lucca: 'The Mickey Mouse Club Was Like a Family.'" Digital Spy. February 13, 2012.

PBS.org. "Sesame Street." Local Kids' TV. http://www.pbs.org/wnet/pioneers-of-television/pioneering-programs/local-kids-tv/.

Sklarewitz, Norman. "Hometown TV Man." *The Rotarian*, June 1955.

Surette, Tim. "CN Real Has Killed the Cartoon Network." TV.com, Aug 21, 2009. http://www.tv.com/news/cn-real-has-killed-the-cartoon-network-17471/.

Wikipedia. "Cartoon Network." http://en.wikipedia.org/wiki/Cartoon_Network.

———. "Disney Channel." http://en.wikipedia.org/wiki/Disney_Channel.

———. "Nickelodeon." http://en.wikipedia.org/wiki/Nickelodeon.

———. "Sarkes Tarzian." http://en.wikipedia.org/wiki/Sarkes_Tarzian.

———. "WTTV." http://en.wikipedia.org/wiki/WTTV.

Woody, Todd. "'Mickey Mouse Club Returns, Minus Much M-I-C-K-E-Y." *Palm Beach Post*, April 23, 1989.

YCDTOTV.com. "Interview with Christine McGlade." http://www.ycdtotv.com/cast/interview.php?cmi=63&p=cmi.

Young, Julie. "Don't Touch That Dial." *Traces of Indiana and Midwestern History*, Summer 2012.

About the Author

Julie Young is an award-winning writer from the Indianapolis area whose work has been featured in a number of local, regional and national publications, including the *Indianapolis Star*, the *Indianapolis Monthly*, the *Indianapolis Business Journal*, *Michiana House & Home*, the *South Bend Tribune*, *ADVANCE for Nurses* magazine, *Catholic Teacher* magazine, the *National Catholic Reporter*, *Evansville Living* and *INTents* magazine. As a former writer with the Associated Press, her work has been seen globally, including on the online juggernaut CNN.com.

Young is also the multi-award-nominated author of five books focusing on local history. Her first book, *A Belief in Providence: A Life of Saint Theodora Guerin*, was a finalist in the Best Books in Indy awards, as well as a nominee for Foreword's Book of the Year award. She followed that up with *Images of America: Historic Irvington*, *Eastside Indianapolis: A Brief History*, *A Brief History of Shelby County*, and *CYO in Indianapolis and Central Indiana*. She has also completed the manuscript for the Indiana Historical Society's Youth Biography series entitled *From Local to Legendary: A Life of Michael Jackson*.

For more information about Young, please visit www.julieyoungfreelance.com.